The Nature Corner

M v Leeuwen and J Moeskops

The Nature Corner

Celebrating the year's cycle with a seasonal tableau

Floris Books

Translated by Polly Lawson

First published in Dutch under the title *De Seiszoenentafel*
by Christofoor Publishers in 1990
First published in English in 1990 by Floris Books

© 1990 by Christofoor Publishers, Zeist
This translation © Floris Books 1990

British Library CIP available

ISBN 0-86315-111-6

Printed in the Netherlands

Contents

Introduction

A seasonal tableau or seasons' table is a place in the home where you can follow the natural cycle of the year. Changes in the natural world are given expression indoors. The figures on the seasons' table depict the essence of what is happening in nature. In attending to the seasonal tableau you will find your observation of what goes on in nature is sharpened. Looking after the table can be absorbing, always alert for something suitable for each season.

This search enables one to live with the rhythm of the spring equinox, summer solstice, autumn equinox, midwinter, and so on. One is no longer simply swept along by the passage of time but consciously experiences the rhythm of the year. This is a source of security.

Young children do not grasp nature intellectually, but unconsciously accept its laws. When we bring the external world indoors, creating a seasonal table in colours and in tableaux without the use of words, children become aware of nature at work in their surroundings.

Older children can help to collect beautiful natural objects for the seasonal tableau. Often they make something themselves which is worthy of a place.

Older children or adults have less need of representation in the form of dolls; a vase with branches or flowers of the season, a print or a beautiful stone is all that is necessary.

All that is needed to create a seasonal tableau is a special table or shelf set apart, or simply somewhere to put the things. It is best to have a particular place which does not change, but gives children a definite focus.

Arranging a seasonal tableau

The basic foundation of a seasonal tableau consists of soft flowing material such as velvet, wool-cotton mix, or silk in appropriate sizes. The fabric can simply be laid on the table, or it can also serve as a background, in which case lift one corner up and tie it to a fixture higher up, varying the height of the background according to the tableau.

A *sky* can be made from a piece of material with a broad hem along one side. Push a length of wire through the hem and bend it to make a semi-circle. Tie string to each end and pull tight to hold the bow in shape (Figure 1).

In a tableau differences of height can be achieved by placing solid objects under the cloth.

The colours of the ground and background are very important because they express the mood of the season (compare the photos of the various seasons' tables in this book). The colour-circle (Figure 2) can be of help here.

Stones, round logs and vases of various sizes are useful for setting up a seasonal table.

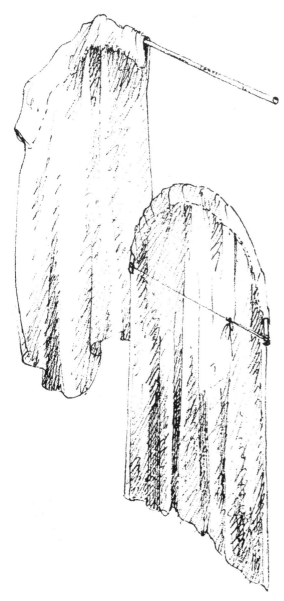

Figure 1. Wire threaded through hem; tie the ends of the string behind the cloth.

The southern hemisphere

In the southern hemisphere the date of Christmas falls at the summer solstice when the midsummer experience is what children are living in, and to follow the suggestions in this book stimulating a northern-hemisphere mood would be disrupting.

There is a special challenge in these parts of the earth to find a way of celebrating the festivals out of the mood of the opposite season. We hope that this book stimulates your own imagination and creativity, so that appropriate tableaux can be created which combine the local seasonal character with the universal timing of the festivals.

Using the seasons' table

The seasonal tableaux in this book reflect particular moments in the year. They were created specially for this book. In your home the seasonal tableau will look different because it will always be changing, with objects coming and going.

Children should be allowed to touch and move the objects on a seasonal table although generally these are not meant to be taken from the table and played with. In our home Mary and Joseph move towards the stable and arrive there at Christmas — an appropriate intervention by children.

There are many figures you will want to make. Mother Earth is the central figure. She can be present all the year round.

Bought things can also be placed on the seasonal table of course — for example: wooden animals, plaster crib figures, chocolate Easter hares, eggs, cut crystal, a candlestick, a postcard or a reproduction. The flowers must

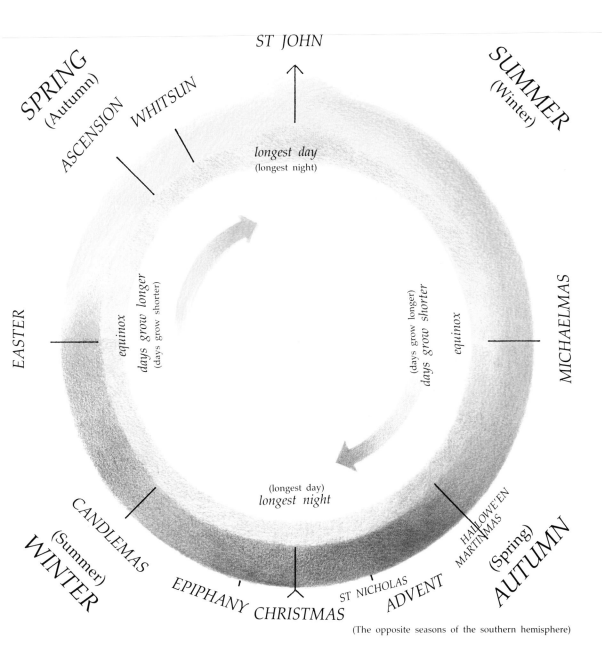

ST JOHN

SPRING (Autumn)

SUMMER (Winter)

ASCENSION

WHITSUN

longest day
(longest night)

EASTER

equinox
days grow longer
(days grow shorter)

(days grow longer)
days grow shorter
equinox

MICHAELMAS

(longest day)
longest night

CANDLEMAS

(Summer)
WINTER

EPIPHANY

CHRISTMAS

ST NICHOLAS

ADVENT

HALLOWE'EN
MARTINMAS

(Spring)
AUTUMN

(The opposite seasons of the southern hemisphere)

Figure 2. Colour circle of the year.

9

be renewed regularly, this also shows the seasons' change.

At all times the tableau should be appropriate to the particular season, and the particular children. For young children it can be dressed much more simply than we have illustrated.

A tableau could also be based on a book relevant to a particular season, for example Elsa Beskow's picture-book, *Ollie's Ski Trip.*

The seasonal tableau forms a good complement to the celebrating of the year's festivals. (Further reading on the meaning of the festivals is in the bibliography.) Becoming more acquainted with the meaning of the festivals will help you to find the right things for the seasonal tableau.

You will find that the results are variable; this can be a challenge to keep trying to improve the tableau.

1. Basic techniques

The dolls in this book are made by various techniques which we shall describe briefly. Of course you can choose any technique for any doll; for example the Spring-Fairy can be made on a stand, the Christmas group can also be made of teased sheep's wool.

Doll made with sheep's wool
(Figure 3)

Well-teased unspun sheep's wool is gently pulled and shaped. The head is formed by making a knot in the wool. This technique is suitable for making figures with little form (see also St Nicholas on page 67).

Marionette (Figure 4)

A marionette has a shaped head (see page 12). The body is formed from the material projecting from the head. Insert a marble or a little stone inside the base of the body to ensure that the marionette hangs vertically. The clothing is loose. Usually the marionette is hung on a wire (see also the Spring-Fairy on page 25).

Standing doll (Figures 23 and 24)

This doll's head is made with knitted cotton (see page 12). The body is formed by firmly stuffing the dress which can be knitted, crocheted, or

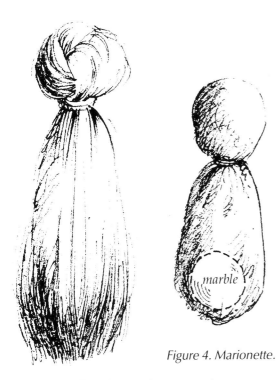

Figure 4. Marionette.

Figure 3. Doll made with sheep's wool.

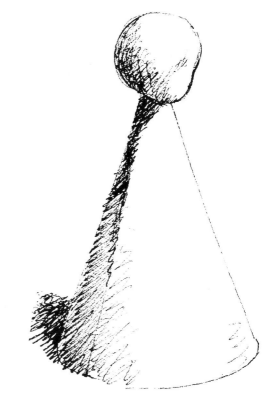

Figure 5. Doll on a cardboard cone.

made of felt. The stuffing is sheep's wool (see also the Flower-Children on page 27).

If the doll will not stand easily you stabilize it: cut out a disc of cardboard and a disc of felt of the same colour and circumference as the bottom of the dress, place the cardboard disc inside the bottom of the dress and sew the felt piece over it on to the edge of the dress.

If necessary the doll can be further stabilized by inserting something heavy, such as a marble or pebbles, before sewing up.

Doll on a cardboard cone
(Figure 5)

This doll's head is also made from knitted cotton (see page 12). The body is made from a semicircular piece of cardboard bent round to form a cone with a hole for the neck. The arms

Doll on a stand (Figure 6)

A doll with a slender figure can have a head (see page 12) set on a wooden stand. The stand is made from a round disc of wood or plywood about 2″ (5 cm) diameter, and a piece of dowelling as thick as a pencil and of the requisite length. Bore a hole in the middle of the disc and glue in the dowelling. Sharpen the other end. About 2″ (5 cm) below the point bore a tiny hole in the stick. This hole is used when fixing the head (Figure 6).

The arms are made of wire bound round with wool. Sew them on at the back. This doll can have clothes made to measure. The doll's figure will depend on how much wool is worked in under the clothing (see also Mother Earth on page 17).

Doll made of wire (Figure 7)

This doll also has a formed head (see page 12). If the doll is to have proper legs and feet, the frame should be made of wire or pipe-cleaner. Wire can be bent more often than pipe-cleaner, but it is not so easily worked (Figure 7).

The shoes can be made of moulded beeswax. However, the doll can easily topple over if it is not stuck to a flat base. To prevent this you could use lead-flashing to line the shoes (Figure 8). Lead-flashing is thin lead used in roofing which can be cut with scissors.

The shoes are made of two layers of lead-flashing, the bottom layer forming the sole. Make a hole in the upper layer with a nail and push the wire of the foot through so that the end of the wire lies between the two layers of lead-flashing. Pull a piece of knitted cotton or felt tightly over the lead to make the shoes and

Figure 6. Doll on a stand.

are made of wire or pipe-cleaners. The clothing is draped on to the figure (Figure 5).

This technique is only suitable for rather shapeless dolls. It is used for the Christmas crib figures for instance, where characterization would be inappropriate.

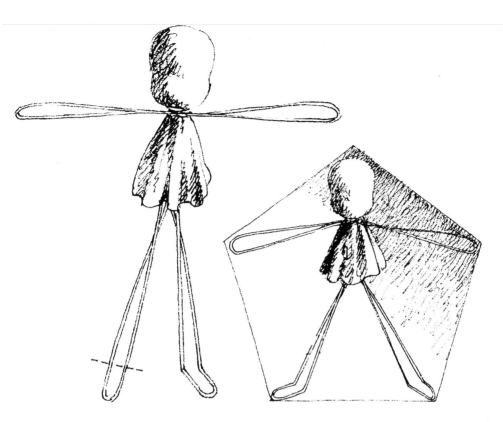

Figure 7. Doll made of wire.

Figure 8. Shoes made of lead flashing.

tie it up round the ankle. (Do not use lead where there are young children, as lead is toxic).

A doll made of wire can be bent into any posture desired (see also the Whitsun-bride on page 42).

Making a doll's head

The head for most of these dolls is made in the following way.

Make a ball by stuffing some clean, teased sheep's wool into a piece of soft thin knitted cotton. Leave some wool sticking out at the neck. Head size is indicated in the pattern, the

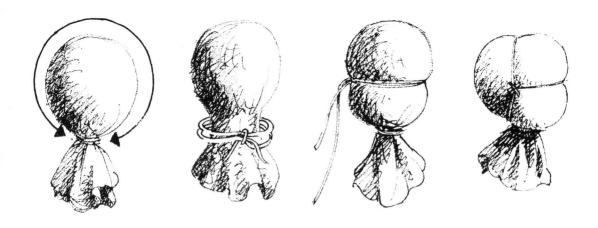

Figures 9–12. Measuring the doll's head. Tying the head. The eye-line. The chin-thread.

measurements being taken over the head, from the neck to the neck (Figure 9).

Tie up the neck firmly using strong thread, for example embroidery thread. This we shall call "tying-up thread". A slip-knot is tied as follows: wind a thread loosely twice round the neck, pass the right end under the left, pass it under both threads and pull tight and tie a knot (Figure 10). With a needle take the ends of the thread right through the head (coming out anywhere) and cut them off close to the material, so the ends are now hidden inside the wool.

To form the eye-line tie a thread around the middle of the ball with the same knot used for tying up the neck. Before knotting, check that the thread is located correctly in middle of the ball and is sufficiently tight to make a depression but not to divide the ball into two parts. Leave the ends of the thread uncut (Figure 11).

Choose the side best suited for the face, bearing in mind where the cheeks and chin are to go, then ease the knot in the thread on the eye-line round to the side (the ear-point).

Once the eye-line has been positioned make a cross-stitch on the ear-point with the ends from the knot. Stick the needle right through the head to the other ear-point, pull the thread fairly tight and make another cross-stitch. Now pass the threads right through the head and cut the ends off. At the back of the head bring the eye-line thread down to the neck to shape the back of the head.

Making a chin-thread will give the head even more form. Make a head as in Figure 11. The longer of the two threads hanging down from the knot on the eye-line is called the working-thread. Bring this under the chin and back up to the eye-line, pass it under the eye-thread and pull it tight, then take it over the middle of the head again back to the first ear-point. Tie the working-thread firmly to the hanging thread at the ear-point. Thread the longer of the two threads and stitch two crosses on top of each other over the ear-point. Pass the needle right through the head to a point exactly opposite. Pull the thread tight so the head becomes

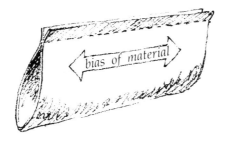
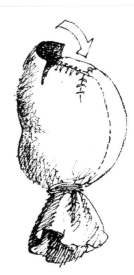

Figures 13–15. Making a nose. Tube of knitted cotton. Finishing the head.

slightly oval and work two cross-stitches over each other. Tease the eye-line at the back of the head down to the base of the head (Figure 12). All the threads are then passed right through the head and cut off.

If the features of the face are to be marked you can make a nose. Sew a little lump of wool or a small bead in the middle of the face just below the eye-line. Check the appearance by covering it with a piece of thicker knitted cotton as you will do to finish the head.

An older face needs a drawn-in mouth. Stick a pin in to mark the position of the mouth. Using strong thread push a long needle in at the corner of the mouth right through the head. Pull the thread out of the needle and rethread the end hanging at the front. Push the needle in again at the other corner of the mouth right through the head. Pull the two ends tight, at the same time checking the front to see that it looks right. Tie the threads together at the back of the head. Pass the ends through the head and cut

them off. If the face is to look older still, use the same technique to create lines running down from the side of the nose past the corners of the mouth and down by the chin (Figure 13).

Once the inside of the head is finished, cover the head with thicker skin-coloured knitted cotton. As not all knitted cotton is equally elastic it is not possible to give exact measurements in the patterns. The rib runs vertically over the head. Measure out a piece which fits tightly around the head in width and is twice as long as the head. Sew this piece into a tube (Figure 14). Turn it and draw it over the head so that at the top there is just enough material to cover the head. Tie a strong thread round the neck. Cut the cloth on the top of the head so that it forms strips which you can lay the flat on the head and sew on securely (Figure 15).

With very small dolls it is not necessary to make an inside head, but proceed as follows:
Make a little tube of thick knitted cotton

(Figure 14), sew across one end and draw tight to close it. Turn the bag inside out and fill with wool. Tie up the neck. Be careful to preserve the proportion of the head to the body.

Finishing off the face

To mark the position of the eyes stick pins in on the eye-line. See if the doll is looking at you! The mouth forms an inverted equilateral triangle with the eyes. Stick a pin in here too. With a coloured pencil draw dots in place of the pins.

The eyes will be more accentuated if you make a depression in the following way. Mark the place of the eyes with pins. Thread a long needle with strong thread. Push the needle into the corner of the eye beside the pin and push it right through the head to the back and pull it through. Unthread the needle. Thread the needle with the thread hanging at the front. Remove the pin. Decide on the width of the eye and insert the needle once again right through the head from the eye-line and pull it through. Form the other eye in the same way. Tighten the four threads and check the effect. Tie the threads but be careful not to pull too hard in case the eyes are too deep. Rethread the ends through the head and cut them off. Now the face can be coloured.

You can give the face rosy cheeks by brushing them with a cloth covered in wax crayon, but be careful not to overdo the effect.

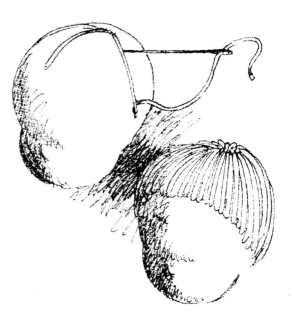

Figure 16. Embroidered hair.

Hair

There are several ways in which you can give dolls hair.

Hair from unspun sheep's wool

White, brown, grey, black or of "fairy-tale wool" which is washed and carded, dyed wool. Place a little tuft of wool on the head and form it to a hair-style. With small stitches sew the wool firmly on to the head using thread of the same colour.

Embroidered hair

For this knitting-wool, embroidery-wool, darning-wool, embroidery thread, mohair, cotton or silk thread can be used.

Decide where the crown of the head is to be and make the first stitch which is a long stitch over the head towards the forehead. Now make a little stitch under the material, and then a long stitch back up to the top again. This second stitch must be a little shorter than the first, otherwise the crown of the head will become too thick. Stitch down to the back of the head and back up again to the top, then down to the ears and back up again (Figure 16). Now the head is divided into four parts. Divide each of these parts into two by stitching down and up in the same manner, and continue in this way until the whole head is filled.

Finally you can finish off with a fringe or long hair for a pony-tail or plaits between the stitched hair.

2. Early spring

Before spring nature still seems to be at rest, but under the surface of the earth there is much activity. This will only become visible in the early spring flowers such as crocuses, hyacinths and narcissi thrusting up through the earth seeking the light.

Children can become more aware of this if you make Mother Earth and her root-children for the seasonal tableau, and tell the story of how Mother Earth wakes them and sets them to work. For weeks the root-children dye and sew their new clothes which must be ready as soon as spring comes. The eager little snowdrop cannot wait and only has time to give her green tassel a little dusting. The daisy who has pricked her finger in the difficult work of cutting and sewing takes care that drops of blood fall only on the underside of the petals.

Mother Earth not only looks after flowers and plants, she also cares for us: she gives us food and sustains us.

Mother Earth

Materials
A piece of soft thin knitted cotton 6″ × 6″ (15 × 15 cm)
Wool
A piece of salmon-coloured thicker knitted cotton 3½″ × 4″ (8.5 × 10 cm)
A wooden stand 6″ (15 cm) high (see page 11)
Wire 16″ (40 cm) long, ¹/₃₂″ (0.8 mm) thick
A scrap of thicker knitted cotton for the hands
Grey unspun wool for the hair

For her clothes you will need material in varying shades of earthy colours.

A round piece of soft cloth 10½" (26.5 cm) diameter for the petticoat

A piece of cloth 8¾" × 6¼" (22 × 16 cm) for the blouse

A piece of cloth 15" × 5½" (38 × 14 cm) for the skirt

A piece of cloth 4¼" × 4¼" (11 × 11 cm) and a tape 8¾" × 1¼" (22 × 3 cm) for the apron

A round piece of cloth 4¼" (11 cm) diameter for the bonnet, or alternatively a piece of cloth 6" × 4¼" (15 × 11 cm) and a tape of 2¼" × ¾" (6 × 2 cm) for a little cap

A scrap of knitted wool for a shawl

A piece of cloth 16" × 8" (40 × 20 cm) for a cloak

A piece of cloth 7" × 7" (18 × 18 cm) of the same colour as the cloak for the hood

12" (30 cm) bias-banding of the same colour as the cloak

Possibly a piece of very thin or wire for the spectacles

A basket

Method

Make a 4¾" (12 cm) head of knitted cotton. This measurement is taken over the head from neck to neck (see page 12).

Mother Earth has a really old face, and so she should be given a nose, and lines round her mouth. After covering the head with thicker knitted cotton the eyes and the mouth can be indented.

Place the head on the stand (see page 11) and tie it on to the stick with the bits of material hanging down from the head. Pass the thread two or three times through the hole in the stand, so that the head is secured. Check the overall height, which must be 7" (18 cm).

Make the *arms* by bending the two ends of the wire back to the middle to make a piece 7" (18 cm) long. Sew the middle of the wire firmly to the back about ½" (1 cm) below the head.

Bind the arms with sheep's wool to fill them out. Mould Mother Earth's bosom with wool too. If the wool will not stay in place it can be secured with a few stitches.

Draw the *hands* as shown in the pattern (Figure 17) on a double thickness of material and sew together on the line. Cut the hands out leaving a small seam and turn them. Pull the hands over the ends of the arms and secure them to the wrists.

Cut out the *petticoat.* Tack round ½" (1 cm) from the edge. Place the stand in the middle of the material and draw up the tacking-thread, gathering the petticoat around the dowelling at waist-height. Secure.

Cut out the *blouse* according to the pattern (Figure 17) adding a small seam allowance. Sew together and cut an opening in the middle of the back. Put the blouse on. Gather the sleeves firmly round the wrists and sew up the slit at the back. Gather the edge of the neck and secure with little stitches.

Cut out the *skirt* according to the measurements given and hem the bottom edge. Sew up the back. Turn the raw edge to the inside and tack a double thread around the top of the skirt. Pull the skirt on over the blouse, pull in the tacking thread and secure.

Hem the *apron* at the sides and bottom. Gather the top. Lay the mid-point of the tape to the mid-point of the apron and sew it on along the top of the apron.

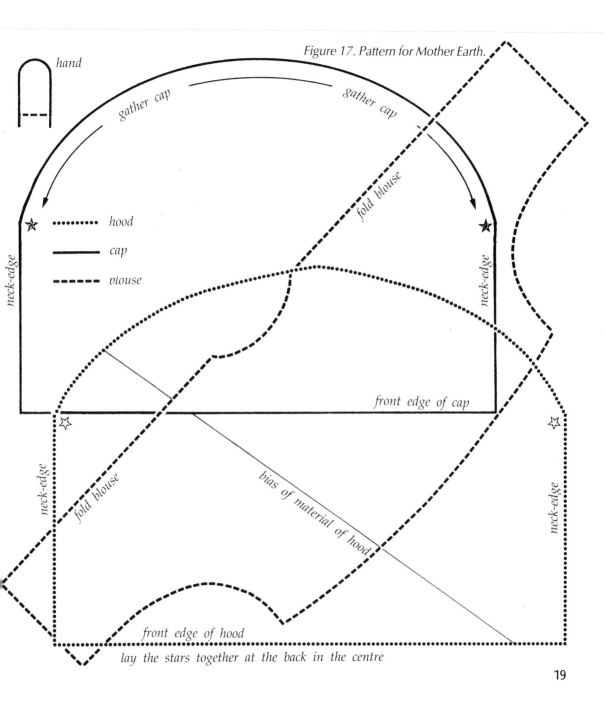

hand

Figure 17. Pattern for Mother Earth.

gather cap   gather cap

fold blouse

••••••••• hood
———————— cap
— — — — vlouse

neck-edge   neck-edge

front edge of cap

neck-edge

fold blouse

bias of material of hood

neck-edge

front edge of hood

lay the stars together at the back in the centre

19

Fold the tape over, turn it in and hem the whole tape. Mother Earth wears her apron for work.

Make the *hair* with grey sheep's wool (see page 16). Make a parting in the middle by fixing the wool with little embroidery stitches. You can make a bun at the back of her head by twisting the wool and stitching it down.

Now Mother Earth is ready for a *cap* or *bonnet* on her head. Cut out the material for the cap according to the pattern (Figure 17). Hem the straight edge which now becomes the front. Tack the round edge and gather this in to the width of the tape 2½" (6 cm). Sew the tape on to the gathers on the right side of the cap. Fold the tape over and hem it on.

For the *bonnet* hem round the piece of cloth. Run a double gathering-thread ¼" (¾ cm) from the edge. Pull in the gathering-thread a little, put the bonnet on the head and pull in the gathering-thread more if necessary. Spread the folds evenly over the bonnet and set it firmly on the head.

For a *knitted shawl* use 3 mm needles.
Cast on 50 stitches.
Knit in moss-stitch for 18 rows, (that is, 1 purl, 1
     plain on each row alternately), decreasing 1
     stitch at the beginning of each row.
Now decrease one stitch at each end 10 times.
12 stitches remain.
Decrease 3 stitches 4 times.
The shawl is now 8" (20 cm) wide and 2¾" (7 cm) at its longest point.

For a *crochet shawl* make a chain to a length of 8" (20 cm). Then make alternately treble and single crochets in continuously decreasing rows so that a piece is made of the same measurements as those of the knitted shawl.

For a *sewn shawl* select a loosely woven material which will drape nicely round the little shoulders. Cut out a piece of the same measurements as the knitted shawl. Hem the shawl all round.

Finally attach a fringe to the diagonal edge of whichever type of shawl you have made. In cold weather Mother Earth can wear her shawl.

When it grows colder Mother Earth wears a *cloak* in which she can wrap herself completely. Cut out the cloak according to the measurements given. Hem the sides and bottom, gather the top.

Cut out the *hood* according to the pattern (Figure 17) with a small seam allowance, note the direction of the bias. Hem the long straight edge. Lay the neck edges together and sew up the round edge.

Lay the gathered edge of the cloak against the neck edge of the hood. Sew together and cover the seam with a bias-binding which extends sufficiently on either side to allow the cloak to be buttoned up.

Figure 18. Crocheted Root-Child.

With a pair of pliers bend the wire to make a little pair of *spectacles.* Place the spectacles on the nose with the side-pieces pushed under the hair.

A tiny basket filled with coloured scraps completes Mother Earth.

Root-Children

Mother Earth's children sleep through the winter under the ground. She wakes them in the early spring. They set to work to make their new clothes as spring comes. Here we shall describe two ways of making the Root-Children.

Crocheted Root-Child (Figure 18)

Materials
Brown knitting wool
Fleece-wool, preferably brown
Brown or yellow mohair wool
A piece of thick knitted cotton 1½" × 1½" (4 × 4 cm)

Method
Make 3 chains, close to a ring and make 5 double-crochets. Next row make 8 double-crochets and increase each row by 3 double-crochets to make a little bag about 2" (5 cm) long. Then crochet in back and forth rows over two thirds of the number of double-crochets to a total length of 2¾" (7 cm). Finally crochet round all stitches decreasing less quickly until the head is closed up. Fill the Root-Child up with wool. Close the fleece wool in the opening with the piece of knitted cotton. Sew the mohair wool in loops round the face with sewing thread. Put a few stitches in the crocheted edge and in the piece of knitted cotton. In this way the cloth will sit evenly. Finally draw in the eyes with a pencil.

Sewn Root-Child

Materials
Fleece-wool
A piece of soft thin knitted cotton 4" × 4" (10 × 10 cm)
A piece of salmon coloured thicker knitted cotton 2¼" (6 cm) wide and 2" (5 cm) long.
A scrap of thicker knitted cotton for the hands
A pipe-cleaner
A piece of dark brown material 7 × 7" (18 × 18 cm).
Wool for the hair
A tablespoonful of rice

Method
Make a 2¾" (7 cm) head with an eye-line (see page 12). Cut out and sew the dress according to the pattern (Figure 19) and turn.

Bend in the pipe-cleaner at both ends so that the arm-piece measures 4" (10 cm) long.

Wind some fleece-wool round the pipe-cleaner. Draw the hands on a double thickness of material according to the pattern. Sew and turn the hands and slide them over the ends of the pipe-cleaner. Secure them on to the wrists.

Sew a tacking thread around the neck-opening of the dress. Fill the dress with the rice. Insert the neck into the neck-opening, pull the tacking-thread tight, tucking the raw edge inwards. Spread out the pleats and set the dress firmly on to the neck.

Stick the arms through the sleeves behind the neck-piece. Gather the edges of the sleeves round the wrists and secure.

Embroider the hair (see page 17), colour the face and set the doll in the required posture.

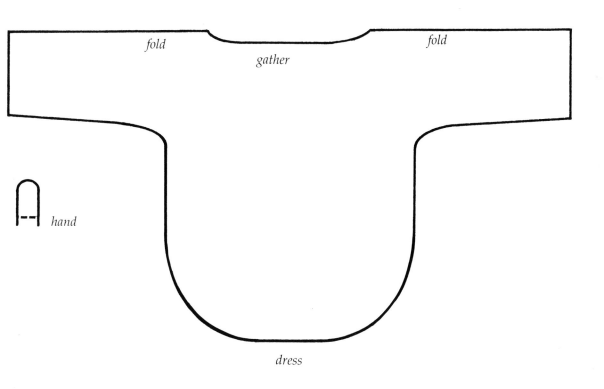

Figure 19. Pattern for sewn Root-Child.

3. Spring

When spring comes this can be represented in a seasonal tableau in the form of a spring-fairy spreading her mantle over the earth. King Winter goes off with his cloak of snow and the dark earth takes on colour again. Spring shows itself particularly in the colours yellow and fresh green. Pink is also a spring colour, which one often sees in the buds of trees and shrubs inside which the green is completely hidden.

It is best to make the spring-fairy out of silk, since it is such a fine material.

The Spring-Fairy

Materials
Fleece-wool
A piece of thin knitted cotton 6″ × 6″ (15 × 15 cm)
A piece of pink thicker knitted cotton 3¼″ × 6″ (8.5 cm × 15 cm)
2 pieces of silk, one 18″ × 18″ (45 × 45 cm), the other 15″ × 15″ (38 × 38 cm)
Embroidery thread
A marble
Light yellow mohair wool or fairy-tale wool
For the head:
A card 6¼″ × 6¼″ (16 × 16 cm)
A piece of silk 7″ × 8½″ (18 × 22 cm)
Bits of tissue-paper in spring colours

Method
Make a 4¾″ (12 cm) head with an eye and chin line (see page 12). Let the knitted cotton project a long way down below the head, as it will form the body.

Hem the two pieces of silk. Laid over each other they make the gown. If the fairy is being made from two differently coloured pieces the darker should be the bigger and should be underneath.

Hem the silk with a thin needle and a silk thread — divided embroidery thread is suitable.

Fold each piece of cloth into four and form a little round hole in the middle by cutting off the thickest corner. Unfold the silk again and lay the cloths diagonally on top of each other so that the points of the uppermost (also the smaller) cloth lie at the centre of each edge of the bottom cloth. Tack with little stitches round the neck-hole. Push the knitted cotton for the fairy's body through, pull in the tacking thread and sew the silk on to the body at the neck.

The points of the uppermost cloth fall in the middle of the front, the middle of the back and on each side. Now the body can be filled with wool. Finally insert the marble and sew up the body. The marble ensures that the fairy hangs the right way up.

For the hair wind the mohair wool about fifty times round a book or a piece of cardboard about 4¼″ (11 cm) wide. Cut the wool through at one side. Lay the strands of wool on top of the head in such a way that they hang down evenly all round and sew them on with little back stitches evenly distributed, so that you get a parting. For the hair you can also use pale yellow fairy-tale wool.

Colour the face.

Now the Spring Fairy can be given some flowers for her hair or a proper fairy hat.

Cut the hat from thin card according to the pattern (Figure 20). Check that the hat will fit the head then stick the hat together. Cut out and fold the silk according to the diagram (Figure 21). Sew the oblique line with the raw edge inwards. Put the card hat inside and glue the raw edge firmly inside the card hat. Hem round the hanging material.

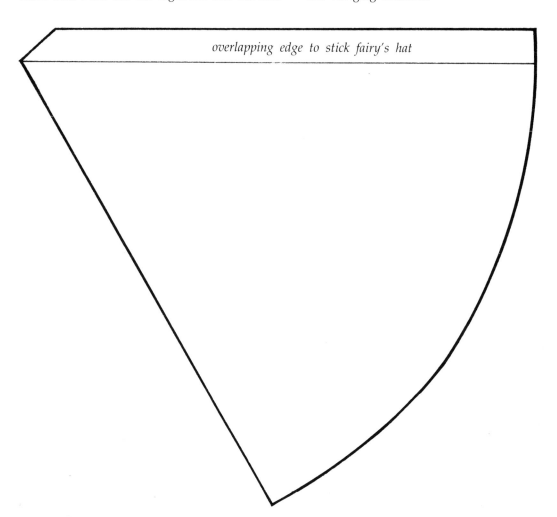

overlapping edge to stick fairy's hat

Figure 20. Pattern for fairy's hat made from card.

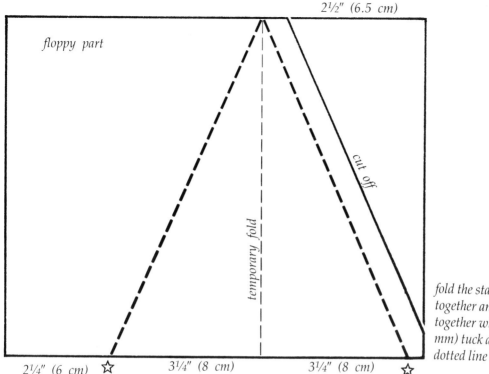

floppy part

2½" (6.5 cm)

temporary fold

cut off

fold the star points together and sew together with a ¼" (5 mm) tuck along the dotted line

2¼" (6 cm) ☆   3¼" (8 cm)   3¼" (8 cm)   ☆

Figure 21. Pattern for fairy's silk hat.

The wreath of flowers is made of little circles of tissue paper about ¾" (2 cm) diameter. Pinch each circle together in the middle. Thread them like beads on a thread with the needle always going through the pinched piece of the flower. Hang the wreath in the fairy's hair, round the hat or round her neck.

Let the fairy float in the air, suspending her by a thread that goes right through her hat, her head and her neck, and is fixed to her body.

Flower-Children

When the Flower-Children come out from below the ground they are quite different in appearance from the Root-Children under the earth. Each evening you can replace a Root-Child with a Flower-Child so that early spring comes to blossom. We shall now describe a number of techniques for making Flower-Children.

Hat and collar

Sometimes the Flower-Children have a hat or collar of petals or green leaves.

As a pattern for petals and leaves use a real flower or an exact copy. Cut the leaves or petals on a strip (leaving them joined on one side of the strip, see Figure 22), or tack and gather them to get more depth in the flower. Such a strip can be fixed round the neck or pulled together to make a hat.

You can make a flat flower by cutting the petals out of a round piece of cloth. This is an alternative hat for some of the Flower-Children. This simple method is more suitable if children are helping.

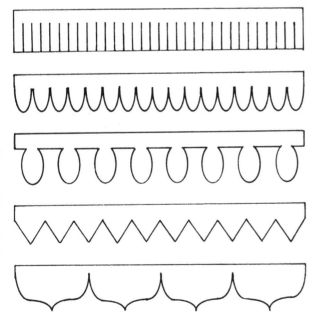

Figure 22. Examples of petals for the Flower-Children.

A flower-hat can be finished off with a centre or a calyx with a little piece of stalk.

For the centre cut out a round or heart-shaped piece of cloth and stick it on the flower or sew it on with embroidery-silk, which makes it look more realistic. You can also stuff a little wool under the centre to make it billow out.

For the *stalk* double a strip of felt and sew.

With some flowers the *base* is only a thickening on the end of the stalk. To achieve this effect roll a strip of felt about ½" (1 cm) wide round the end of the stalk and sew on.

Sometimes the base is a calyx which is made in the same way as a flower-calyx: tack a strip of felt and gather it. There are endless ways in which the cutting can be done (Figure 22). Make sure that the number of petals is right for the flower you are making.

A Flower-Child made of teased sheep's wool

This is a very simple Flower-Child which can be made by children.

Materials
6" (15 cm) teased sheep's wool pulled to the
    thickness of a finger
A strip of felt 2¼" × 4¾" (6 × 12 cm)
Scraps of felt for the petals
Embroidery thread

Method
Tie a knot in the middle of the piece of sheep's wool to make the doll's head. Choose one side for the face. Make a cloak by gathering the strip of felt along the longer side and fitting it around the wool "doll", close it round the neck. Sew a flower-hat on to the head.

Figure 23. Flower-child of teased sheep's wool.

Scraps of felt for the hat, green combined with
    another colour
Embroidery-thread in suitable colours

Method
Make a very simple 2¼″ (6 cm) head without
wool in the neck.
    The dress is knitted in one piece.
Cast on 14 stitches.
Knit in moss-stitch (1 plain, 1 purl on each
    needle alternately) for 24 rows.
Cast on 4 stitches at each end for the arms (22
    stitches).
Over the centre 8 stitches knit one row plain,
    one row purl for 10 rows while continuing
    to knit the sleeves in moss-stitch.

A knitted Flower-Child

Materials
Fine knitting cotton in the appropriate flower
    colour.
2.5 mm knitting needles
Fleece wool
A piece of thicker knitted cotton 2″ × 2″ (5 × 5
    cm)
A scrap of thicker knitted cotton for the hands
Wool for the hair
A pipe-cleaner

Figure 24. Knitted Flower-Child.

In the next row cast off the centre 2 stitches
loosely and in the following row cast them
on again thus forming the neck.
Continue for 10 rows.
Cast off 4 stitches at each end (14 stitches).
Knit 24 rows in moss-stitch.
Cast off.

Sew the arm and side seams. Insert the neck
into the neck-hole and sew the dress on to the
neck.

Bend in the pipe-cleaner at each end to make
a length of 3" (8 cm). Wind a little tuft of wool
round the pipe-cleaner. Draw the hands
according to the pattern (Figure 25) on a double
thickness of material. Sew and turn the hands
and draw over then ends of the pipe-cleaner.
Sew them on to the wrist. Push the arms along
the sleeve-openings behind the neck piece.
Secure the sleeves at the wrists.

Fill the doll from below with fleece wool so
that it can stand. Give the Flower-Child a waist
by tacking an embroidery thread through the
line between the stocking-stitch and the moss-
stitch.

Finish off the Flower-Child by giving her hair
and a hat or collar of petals (see Figures 23 and
24).

A crocheted Flower-Child

Materials
Fine knitting cotton
A suitable crochet-hook
Fleece wool
A piece of thicker knitted cotton 2" × 2" (5 × 5
cm)
A scrap of thicker knitted cotton for the hands
Wool for the hair
Scraps of felt for the petals

Method
Make a very simple 2¼" (6 cm) head without
wool in the neck (see page 12). The dress is
crocheted from the top downwards.
Make 12 chains and close them to a ring with a
half double-crochet. Work double-crochet on
to this and increase 2 double-crochets in the
next 5 rows, so that you have 22 double-
crochets altogether. Continue crocheting till
you have reached the required length (8 to 10
rows). Fasten off. Work the neck-piece into the
neck-opening of the dress and secure it. Fill the
dress with fleece wool so that the doll can
stand. Make petals round the neck (see page
28).

For the cap make 3 chains, close to a ring and
increase the next 3 rows 5 double-crochets
each time so that you have altogether 18
double-crochets. Make 5 more rows and fasten
off. Put hair on the head and sew on the cap.

A Flower-Child with a flower in her hand

Materials
Fleece wool
A piece of soft thin knitted cotton 4" × 4" (10 ×
10 cm)
A piece of pink thicker knitted cotton 4¾" long
and 2¼" wide (12 × 6 cm)
A scrap of thicker knitted cotton for the hands
A pipe-cleaner
2 pieces of felt (green or of the colour of the
flower), one 4¾" × 2⅛" (12 cm × 5.5 cm)
(the skirt) and 2" × 3½" (9 × 5 cm) (the
top-piece)
Wool for the hair

Method
Make a 2¾" (7 cm) head with an eye-line (see
page 12). Cut out the top-piece of the dress

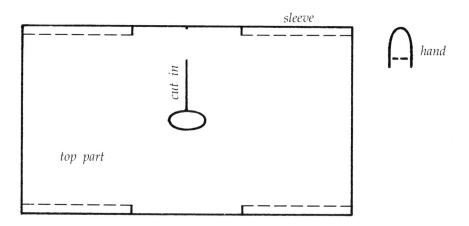

Figure 25. Pattern for Flower-Child.

according to the pattern (Figure 25). Sew up the seams of the sleeves. Sew the centre back seam of the skirt and gather the top edge. Sew the skirt on to the top-piece, so that the centre back seams are aligned as are the centre front points. Bend in the ends of the pipe-cleaner so that the arm-piece is 4″ (10 cm) long. Wind some fleece wool round the pipe-cleaner. Draw the hands according to the pattern (Figure 25) on a double thickness of material. Sew and turn the hands and draw them over the ends of the pipe-cleaner. Secure them round the wrists.

Push the neck into the neck-opening.

Push the arms through the sleeves behind the neck-piece. Sew up the dress. You can also secure it at the neck and wrists. Fill the skirt up with wool so that it can stand. Make the hair as described on page 16. Colour the face.

Felt dandelions

To make a felt flower use a real flower or a drawing as a pattern. You can of course make other flowers than the dandelion.

Materials
Two green pipe-cleaners (or dye two white
    pipe-cleaners with green water-colour)
2 pieces of felt in two close shades of yellow:
    the darker yellow 1″ × 3″ (2.5 × 8 cm) and
    the lighter yellow 1″ × 4¾″ (2.5 × 12 cm)
Green felt

Method
Cut into the yellow felt along the long side with the cuts very close together (about 1 mm). Take care as it is easy to spoil the felt while cutting in this way. Twist the darker strip first round the end of the pipe-cleaner. Fix it with a spot of glue

Figure 26. A dandelion leaf.

4. Easter

Easter brings longer hours of daylight to gladden our hearts, and in a sheltered spot the warmth of the sun can once again be felt. Spring flowers bring colour. The buds on the trees show that the leaves will soon emerge. The birds are singing and the lambs are frisking in the fields. Spring brings great joy; it is good to pause and consider for a moment. Children enter happily into all the new young life, into all that seemed so dead but was not so. For adults nature shows the picture of resurrection, the true Easter festival. On the seasonal tableau you can express this resurrection by using garden cress, eggs, chicks, lambs and the Easter hare.

or a few stitches. Then twist the second strip round it and secure this too.

From a strip of green felt make the base of the flower round the stalk underneath the yellow petals.

Cut the leaf as shown in the sketch (Figure 26) or copy a real dandelion leaf. Sew the second pipe-cleaner on to the leaf, as a central vein. Bend the leaf a little and the vein will come to the back.

Join the flower-stalk and the leaf-stalk together underneath. The Flower-Child can now hold the flower.

Figure 27. Hen with chicks.

Hen with chicks

Just imagine that you had never seen an egg. The thing looks like a stone and seems to be dead. How amazing to see a little chick come creeping out of it. From what appeared dead something living issues forth. The chick represents what is new.

Hen (Figure 27)

Materials
Crochet hook No. 3
Suitable wool
Fleece wool
Red felt
Thick black thread

Method
Make 3 chains and close to a ring. Work 5 double-crochets into this chain. Into each double-crochet now work 2 double-crochets and continue till there are 20 double-crochets. Then work 1 double-crochet into each double-crochet (that is once round the ring). Now work 2 double-crochets into the next 4 double-crochets and 1 double-crochet into the fifth double-crochet. Repeat 3 times (36 double-crochets). Then work 12 rows of double-crochets counting from the middle. For the neck crochet over 12 double-crochets continuously going round, that is not back and forth. The neck is 5 rows high. Now keep on working 2 double-crochets together until there are no stitches left.

Fill the hen with wool and sew up the back. For the wings make 4 chains and then 3 double-crochets. Do not go back but continue to crochet along the bottom of the piece, 1 double-crochet in the base chain and 3 double-crochets in the other side of the chains. Then crochet twice more round, increase at the short sides so that the wing stays flat. Crochet the second wing in the same way. Sew on both wings to the sides of the hen's body with two stitches at the front. Make the eyes with knot-stitches (that is, make a little stitch, twist the thread a few times round the needle, pull through and fasten at the same place). Cut out a beak, a comb and two gills from the felt and sew them on to the right places.

Chicks

Materials
3 mm knitting needles
Suitable wool
A thick black thread
Orange felt

Method
Cast on 20 stitches.
Knit garter stitch (all plain) for 3 rows.
On every following row knit the first two
    stitches together.
Continue until there are 4 stitches left.
Pass these 4 stitches on to a thread and sew the
    diagonal sides together.
Fill the chick with fleece wool and sew up the bottom (if you leave the bottom open instead of the wool you can put in a chocolate egg).
Give the chick eyes and a beak like the hen.

Hares

Traditionally hares belong to Easter because of their selfless manner of life: it is said that when a hare is being hunted and grows tired another hare will take over his part and run out in front of the huntsman. According to another ancient tradition the Easter Hare brings new seeds of life in the form of eggs.

A woolly hare

Materials
Brown knitting wool
Brown felt
2 black beads

Method

The hare is made from three woolly balls.

The ball is made from very short strands of wool bound together in the middle. The more strands the better the ball. Catch a 10″ (25 cm) long strand between the ring-finger and the middle finger of your left hand. With your right hand wind wool round the closed fingers of the left hand holding the hand properly flat. When enough wool is fully wound on tie up the middle with the loose strand which you have been holding in the left hand. Slide the whole thing carefully off your fingers. Cut open the loops. Shake out the pumpkin and cut off the strands sticking out.

In the same way make a ball over three fingers for the head and another over two fingers for the tail.

Sew the head on to the biggest woolly ball.

Cut the bottom flat so that the hare will stand.

Sew the tail on as low down as possible. Cut out two ears from the felt and sew them on to the head. Sew the two beads on where the eyes should be and pull them into the head so far that they can just be seen in the fluff.

For bigger or smaller hares borrow a man's hand or a child's hand: or substitute a piece of cardboard.

Felt hare

Materials
A piece of felt 5½″ × 7″ (14 × 18 cm) the
    colour of a hare
A piece of pink felt
Fleece wool
2 black beads
Thin knitting wool for the tail

Method

Cut all the pattern parts out of felt, omitting seams (Figure 28). The whole animal is sewn together with button-hole-stitch. Lay the two parts of the body on to each other and sew from the stuffing-opening along the back to the neck. Sew the head mid-piece between the head-pieces. Sew a little piece under the chin up to the patch in front. Lay the bottom-piece against the body and sew it on. Stuff the hare firmly with wool and sew up the filling-opening. Button-hole stitch together a brown and a red ear. Fold the ear over lengthwise with the pink side in. Sew the bottom of the ear on to the head with the fold to the back. Make the second ear in the same way. Do not cut off the thread, but thrust the needle through the head to the place where the eye should come. Thread on a bead and push the needle through the head to the place of the other eye. Thread the second bead and push through to the first ear. Pull the thread tight so that the beads are lying in the material. Fasten off firmly where the ear was sewn on. If you wish, make some whiskers with embroidery silk.

Make a tiny ball of thin wool and sew it on for a tail.

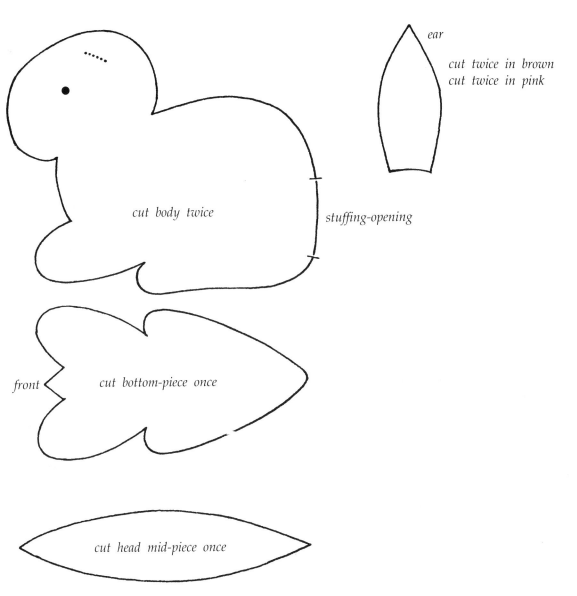

ear

cut twice in brown
cut twice in pink

cut body twice

stuffing-opening

front

cut bottom-piece once

cut head mid-piece once

Figure 28. Pattern for a hare.

35

Sheep with lambs

Materials
White felt
Fleece wool
2 pipe-cleaners 2¾" (7 cm) long
Tufts of good washed sheep's wool
2 small beads

Method
Cut out pattern parts for a sheep (Figures 29 and 30) omitting seams. Lay the leg mid-piece between the two parts of the sheep. Sew with button-hole stitch. Wind some fleece-wool round the pipe-cleaners. Insert both ends of one pipe-cleaner into the forelegs and both ends of the other into the hindlegs. Sew up from the breast upwards over the head to point A. Join the head mid-piece left and right to point B. Now sew from point C to half way down the back before finishing the ears. Stuff the head tightly with wool. Turn in the mid-piece at the back of the head to the dotted line D. Sew the dotted line D on to the sheep at point C. This makes the ears. Stuff the body and sew up. Lay a good tuft of fleece-wool on the sheep's back and sew it on here and there with little stitches. Repeat this till the sheep has a good fleece. Some sheep have woolly heads.

With a fine needle fasten a thread at the neck. Push the needle through to the eye-socket. Thread on a bead push through to the place of the other eye. Thread the second bead and push through back to the neck. Pull the thread so that the eyes are pulled slightly into the head.

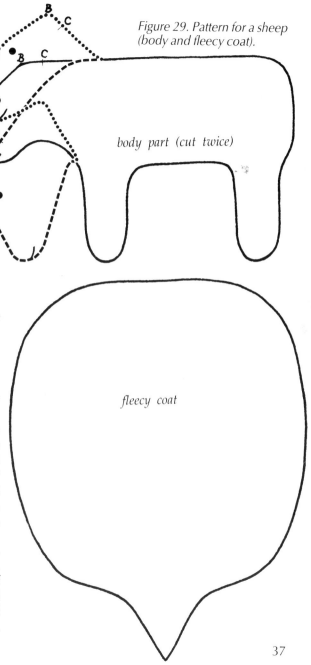

Figure 29. Pattern for a sheep (body and fleecy coat).

body part (cut twice)

fleecy coat

37

Fasten off securely. Work a few stitches for the mouth.

Instead of loose wool you could give the sheep a coat of fleecy woollen fabric (Figure 29).

The illustration shows sheep in various postures. They are all made in the same way. The lambs are smaller. They have a 2" (5 cm) long pipe-cleaner and little or no wool sewn on.

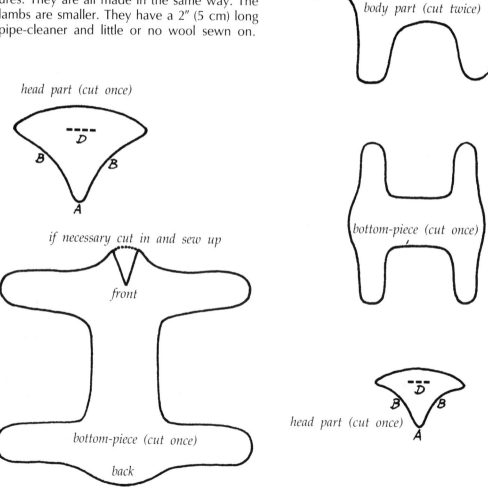

body part (cut twice)

head part (cut once)

if necessary cut in and sew up

front

bottom-piece (cut once)

back

bottom-piece (cut once)

head part (cut once)

Figure 30. Pattern for a sheep (leg mid-piece and head mid-piece).   Figure 31. Pattern for a lamb.

5. Ascension and Whitsun

Forty days after Easter comes Ascension Day. The blossoms seem to reach to the sky. The pollen even further. The buds are opening and the trees are turning green. The earth seems to breathe out. Nature is enticing us out of doors. Flowers appear on the banks and in the meadows. On the seasonal tableau the flower-children can constantly bring new kinds of flowers.

Ten days after Ascension and fifty days after Easter is the festival of Whitsun.

We suggest that at Whitsun the seasonal tableau can be decorated with paper flowers. It may seem strange that just when nature is giving us so many flowers we use paper flowers, but the festival of Whitsun encourages us to work and to create. Paper is a material which lends itself well to this. We can easily be inventive. You will be amazed at your own ingenuity. You should not in fact be working according to a pattern, so we shall only give some basic indications.

Paper is not very durable, and certainly will not last in a sunny room. However, it is not a bad thing if the paper turns yellow. Next year it will be Whitsun again and we hope that we shall have found new inspirations.

Paper flowers

Materials
Tissue paper or crêpe paper
Scissors, adhesive, adhesive tape
Thin wire or wire-thread
Cane, wire or twigs as stalks

Method
Winding on technique. Stick a strip of paper (which can be incised or not) firmly on to the top of the stalk with glue, adhesive tape or wire. By turning the stalk a flower is twisted. You can twist variously coloured and variously incised strips. For ways of incising see page 28.

When twisting the paper it can be pleated against the stalk giving more room to the calyx. The base of the flower can be fixed by winding wire or wire-thread round it.

Pinching-technique. Pinch a piece of paper together in the middle and you will get a flower. Try out various forms and sizes or different layers on top of each other. You can attach these flowers easily to the stalk with adhesive tape or with thin wire.

Pleating technique. Make a pile of little papers of one colour or of harmonizing shades. You

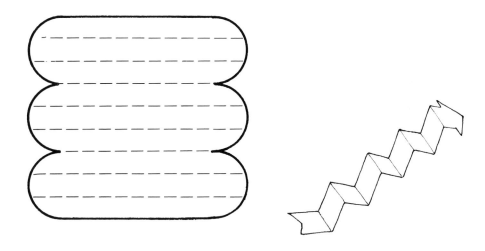

Figure 32. Folding technique for petals.

can also cut into the two sides facing each other. Fold the whole pile together like a concertina (Figure 32) and fasten it by passing a piece of wire round it and twisting it together. This wire can also make the stalk. Now very carefully draw the various layers upwards one by one.

Finishing off. These flowers can be stuck without stems on to a wreath which is made of green paper wrapped round. However if they are to be put into a vase you should ensure that they have nice stems. Wrap them with a narrow strip of green paper securing it with a spot of glue at the base. As you wind on you can glue on a leaf here and there. You could also use loose green sprigs as a basis for the bouquet.

Whitsun doves

The white dove of peace is the messenger from heaven. Draw a beautiful dove yourself or use the pattern in Figure 33. Cut the body out of white card. Draw in an eye on each side. Make a little hole for the thread to hang it by and a slit for the wings.

The wings can be made of various kinds of materials: a piece of tissue-paper, thin silver card, thin white paper or a paper doily.

The wings are about $2^{3}/4'' \times 5''$ (7 × 13 cm). They are folded together like a concertina and inserted through the slit extending equally on each side. Fan them out nicely. Hang the dove on a thread above the seasonal tableau.

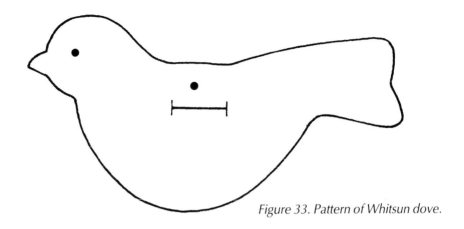

Figure 33. Pattern of Whitsun dove.

The Whitsun couple

There is an old custom in the Netherlands that at Whitsun the Whitsun-Bride is decked with paper flowers and tinkling bells while standing under an arch adorned with flowers and greenery. The bridal train then processes through the village.

You can illustrate any of these customs on the seasonal tableau. We shall describe how to make the Whitsun couple.

The bride

Materials
Fleece wool
A piece of thin knitted cotton $4^1/4'' \times 4^1/4''$ (11 × 11 cm)
a piece of thicker knitted cotton $2^1/4'' \times 2^1/4''$ (6 × 6 cm)
a scrap of thicker knitted cotton for the hands
Wire 2 ft. (60 cm) long, $^1/32''$ (0.8 mm) thick
a piece of white silk cloth for the dress $8'' \times 6^1/4''$ (20 × 16 cm)
a piece of lace $4^3/4''$ (12 cm) for the collar

a piece of soft white material for her pantaloons $4^1/4'' \times 3^1/2''$ (11 × 9 cm)
8 ft (2.5 m) light yellow mohair wool
Embroidery silk for her hair-ribbon and for trimming the dress
2 pieces of white beeswax the size of a marble for the shoes.

Method
Make a $2^3/4''$ (7 cm) head with an eye-line (see page 12) and make embroidered hair (see page 17).

The foundation of the body is made with wire. Cut a piece of wire $12^1/2''$ (32 cm) long for the body and the legs, and a piece 11" (28 cm) long for the arms. Bend the wire according to the diagram (see Figure 34) Attach the arms to the body by winding the loose ends round the body. Wrap the skeleton thinly in wool. For the feet leave $^1/2''$ (1 cm) free at the bottom of the legs.

The head can now be set in its place. Cut a slit on each side of the material of the neck piece, pull it down at the front and back of the skeleton and tie it firmly under the arms. Fold the thicker knitted cotton double for the hands which you draw as shown in the pattern (Figure 35). Sew them, cut them out and turn them. Place them on the ends of the wire. Tie the hands round the wrists firmly.

Cut out the pantaloons and the dress according to the pattern (Figure 35) allowing a small seam and sew them. Hem the dress with embroidery-stitches. Put the pantaloons on the doll. Secure the top of the pantaloons under the armpits. Gather the neck of the dress leaving the thread to hang. Put the dress on the doll. Pull in the gathering thread, spread out the folds of the dress and secure the neckband firmly round the neck. Tack the cuffs, turn the raw edges in, pull in the tacking-thread and secure the cuffs at the wrists.

Gather the lace collar and secure round the neck. Bend 1/2" (1 cm) wire forwards at the bottom of the legs. Work the wax soft and form the shoes round the wire (see pattern, Figure 36). Make sure that the soles are flat so that the bride can stand. Gather in the bottoms of the pantaloon-legs making sure that they fall nicely over the shoes.

Round the head plait a wreath of three strands of embroidery thread 6¾" (17 cm) long, tie the ends together and let these hang down unplaited. Embroider little flowers on it with blanket-stitches.

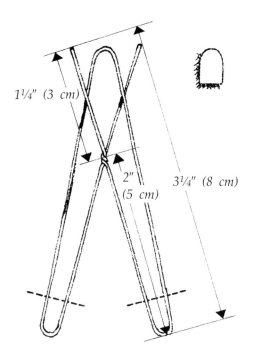

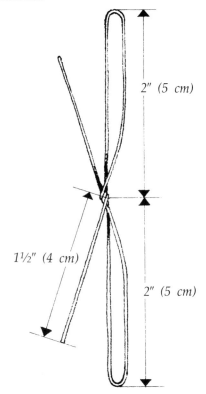

Figure 34. Bending pattern for wire.

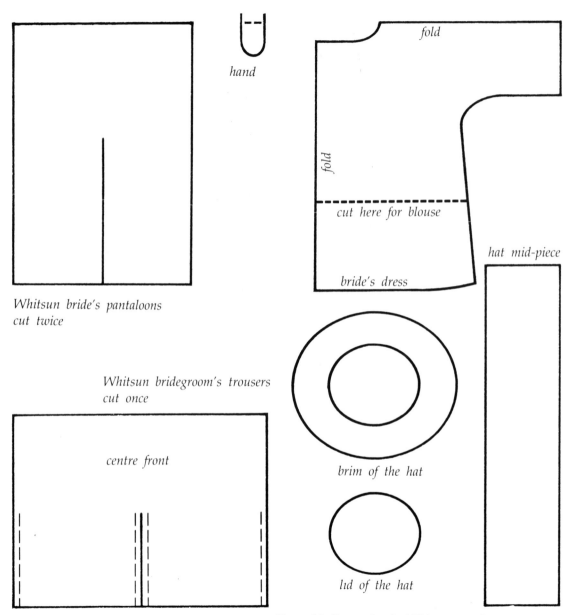

hand

fold

fold

cut here for blouse

bride's dress

Whitsun bride's pantaloons
cut twice

hat mid-piece

Whitsun bridegroom's trousers
cut once

centre front

brim of the hat

lid of the hat

Figure 35. Pattern for the Whitsun couple.

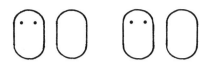

Figure 36. Feet of the Whitsun couple.

A bouquet of roses

For each rose take a strip of tissue-paper ³/₄″ × 2¹/₄″ (2 × 6 cm)

Fold in half along the length. Take the strip with the fold uppermost between the thumb and forefinger of your left hand (Figure 37). Make the rose by gradually rotating the strip with the thumb and forefinger of your right hand, so that the base becomes the open rose and the folded edge forms the base of the flower. Twist the base together and put a drop of glue on it. Now take a round piece of green tissue-paper about 1″ (2.5 cm) diameter. Hold it in the middle and stick the rose in it. The stem is made from a piece of tissue-paper ¹/₂″ × 1¹/₄″ (1.5 × 3 cm) twisted round the point of the base.

A couple of these roses make a bouquet which is then sewn into the hand of the bride.

The bridegroom

Materials
Fleece wool
A piece of thin knitted cotton 4¹/₄″ × 4¹/₄″ (11 × 11 cm)
A piece of thicker knitted cotton 2¹/₄″ × 2¹/₄″ (6 × 6 cm)
A scrap of thicker knitted cotton for the hands
Wire 2 ft. (60 cm) long, ¹/₃₂″ (0.8 mm) thick
8 ft (2.5 m) yellow mohair wool for the hair
A piece of white silk cloth for the shirt 4¹/₄″ × 6¹/₄″ (11 × 16 cm)

A bit of lace 4³/₄″ (12 cm) for the collar
Pieces of felt for the trousers and the hat about 3″ × 4³/₄″ (8 × 12 cm)
A scrap of silk for the stockings
2 bits of beeswax the size of a marble for the shoes
Bamboo skewers
Embroidery thread
Tiny bells or beads

Method
Make the foundation of the bridegroom in the same way as that of the bride.

Cut out the shirt according to the pattern (Figure 35) allowing a small seam and sew it. Gather the neck edge of the shirt. Put the shirt on the doll and pull in the gathering-thread, spread out the folds of the shirt and secure the neckband to the neck. Gather the cuffs turning the raw edges in, pull in the tacking-thread and secure the sleeves to the wrists. Gather the lace collar and secure it to the neck.

Figure 37. Roses made of tissue paper.

The stockings are made by winding a piece of silk round the calves, turning the raw edges in on to the calves and securing with little stitches. Leave 1/2" (1 cm) of the leg free at the bottom for the foot.

Cut out the felt trousers without seam allowance. Sew up the inside leg seams. Put the trousers on the bridegroom. Tuck the shirt in nicely. With a tuft of wool give him side-whiskers and sew up the centre back-seam. Gather the trousers at the waist and secure.

Bend the bottom of the wire of the legs 1/2" (1 cm) to the front. Knead the wax till it is soft and form the shoes round the wire so that the stockings go into the shoes. Make sure that the soles are flat so that the bridegroom can stand (see pattern, Figure 36).

Cut out the felt hat according to the pattern (Figure 35) without seam allowance. Sew it together and set it on the head.

Make a bauble from a bamboo skewer with little bells on threads at the top. Sew the bauble on to the bridegroom's hand.

The archway of roses

Materials
Wire 36" (90 cm) long, 1/32" (0.8 mm) thick
Green tissue-paper 3/4" (2 cm) wide and as long
    as possible
A number of roses without leaves and stem as
    described for the bride's bouquet (see 32).

Method
Bend the two ends of the wire back to the middle to give a total length of 18" (45 cm). Twist the wire together and make a nice arch. Make cuts into one side of the tissue-paper along the whole length, each cut being a little more than halfway across. Lay the strip of paper with the cut side uppermost on to the wire and wind it spirally round the wire. Continue until the whole arch is covered.

Stick the roses on to the front of the arch. Bend the feet of the arch 3/4" (2 cm) forwards so that a pebble or stone can be balanced on them to make the arch stand.

6. St John's Tide

According to the calendar summer begins when the days have ceased to grow longer. The sun is at its highest point. The trees are in full leaf. The flowers give forth scent. The butterflies are fluttering around. Everything that was asleep in the earth during the winter has now emerged. All is green. Then comes the night of St John, the night when Nature celebrates her festival and wonderful things happen — a Midsummer-night's dream. The sun entices us out of doors, and lets us forget our everyday cares. This is just a brief interlude, however, for already we must resume our daily pattern. Imperceptibly we are moving towards autumn: the first fruits have already been gathered in, gradually the days grow shorter.

Beehive with bees

However far bees fly out to search for honey, they always return to the hive with their treasure.

Beehive

Materials
A fluffy kind of cord
A good reel of strong thread

Method
Make a little coil at the beginning of the cord. Sew it up. Pull in the coil tight to make it as small as possible. Make stitches over the coil to bind it together. Work on down the hanging cord,

Figure 38. Beehive.

47

each time stitching it into the round of the coil which is already sewn on and in this manner make a convex mat (Figure 38). When the hive is wide enough, work almost straight down to produce a hive like that shown in the illustration. Widen the hive slightly at the bottom so that it will stand firmly.

Bees

Materials
Catkins saved from the previous season
White tissue-paper
Dark yellow knitting wool

Method
Make the bee's body by winding the wool about four times round the catkin. Cut off the ends of the wool and stuff them into the scales of the catkin. Cut the wings from tissue-paper following sketch (Figure 39).

Lay the wings on to the body and tie a thread round them from which you can suspend them. The wings will now be drawn into the scales of the catkin. Spread them out carefully. Cut off the short end of the thread.

You can hang the bees on a ring of about 4" (10 cm) diameter. Make the suspension threads of different lengths so that the whole thing looks like a swarm. Make some bees without suspension threads as well and pin them on or near the hive.

Figure 39. Bees' wings.

Summer fairies

Materials
12" (30 cm) white well-teased sheep's wool ¾" (2 cm) wide
4¼" (11 cm) white well-teased sheep's wool ¾" (2 cm) wide
16" (40 cm) ribbon
A piece of silk cloth 8" × 4¼" (20 × 11 cm)

Method
Tie a knot in the middle of the 12" (30 cm) teased sheep's wool and lay the ends together. The knot makes the head. Tie off the neck with the ribbon, tying the knot behind leaving the ends hanging. Lay the 4¼" (11 cm) wool (for the arms and wings) between the two strips of wool under the head. Cross both the left-hand and the right-hand ribbon over the chest. Cross them behind at the waist and then in front at the waist and finally tie a knot at the centre-back. Divide the cross-pieces into two pieces, the first for the arms. Moisten your fingers and twist the wool together to make the wrist. The second piece is for the wings which you fluff out well behind the arms. Fluff the skirt well out and let it come to a point.

Fold the piece of silk into four and in one cutting round off the four corners. Tack the cloth over the middle of the long side. Pull in the tacking thread until the pleats in the middle are ½" (1 cm) wide all together. Sew the silk wings on to the fairy's back passing the thread up through the head so that the fairy can be suspended by it.

Figure 40. Wreath made of grass.

Grass

Long stalks of grass can decorate the seasonal tableau. See how many different kinds of flowering grasses you can find. They can be put in a vase as a bouquet, laid on the table or stuck into a potato (first make holes in the potato with a thick needle).

You can also plait long grass. Take three stalks or thin bundles and plait them together. The ends of the plait can be tied together with a flat knot, or bound together with another stalk to make a wreath. A wreath can be adorned with flowers inserted into it (Figure 40).

It is possible to make dolls of grass. The best results are obtained when the grass is still moist. Take a bunch of grass as thick as your finger. Bend it double and tie it up with a stalk or a piece of string. The part tied off forms the head. The arms are formed by laying a thinner bunch of grass between the two bunches under the head. Tie round the waist. Make the hands by tying the arms at the wrists. The woman is now finished. A man is formed by tying off legs the same way as the arms.

7. Summer

During the summer holidays the seasonal tableau often receives much less attention. A cloth the colour of straw and fresh flowers, are often all that is required. Beautiful things found by chance or something made by a child can be placed on the seasonal tableau. Even a dead bee can be put on the table to be examined and admired at close quarters as can shells, pebbles, little sticks, mosses, or anything that merits close attention.

When the weather is wet or very hot it is pleasant to be indoors with children making things from treasures found outside. Here are some suggestions.

A mosaic of shells

A sand-castle (add a little starch to the wet sand to make it stiffer, see Figure 41)

Little boats of bark and twigs with a leaf for a sail,

A stick nicely carved with a knife

Little birds with feathers stuck into a body of beeswax or a fir-cone.

Swans made of a pipe-cleaner with white feathers glued on and a beak of beeswax.

A pond made of a glass plate with a blue cloth under it.

With all the busy activities of the holidays work at the seasonal tableau can be an oasis of peace.

Figure 41. Sand-castle.

8. Autumn

Summer draws to its end. As at Easter, day and night are again about the same length. After Easter the days were longer than the nights, light had the upper hand. Then the plants and trees were growing; there came leaf, blossom and the beginnings of fruition. Now it is time to consider what autumn brings. On to the seasonal tableau come fruit and seed. The tender rose of spring has ripened to a deep red and now is turning brown. As nature decays, the human being must have the courage to persevere. In order to strengthen this courage we celebrate the festival of St Michael on September 29. Old pictures show the Archangel Michael fighting the dragon. He is also depicted holding scales. What Michael teaches us is to have the courage to maintain our stand when nature is apparently dying, and to grapple with our own dragon-nature and to tame it.

You can imitate a dragon with chestnut husks (Figure 42) on the seasons' table; having the courage to take the whole prickly fruit, not just the smooth conkers.

A pumpkin child

Materials
A piece of soft thin knitted cotton 4³/₄″ × 4³/₄″ (12 × 12 cm)
Fleece-wool
A piece of thicker knitted cotton 2¹/₄″ × 2³/₄″ (6 × 7 cm)

Figure 42. Dragon made of chestnut husks.

A round piece of orange flannel 7″ (18 cm) diameter
Orange knitting wool or fairy-tale wool for the hair
Scraps of green felt: 4″ × 1″ (10 × 2.5 cm) for the collar; 3″ × ³/₈″ (8 × 1 cm) for the stalk

Method
Make a simple 3¹/₂″ (9 cm) head (see page 12). With orange thread tack round ¹/₂″ (1 cm) from the edge of the round piece of flannel. Pull in the tacking-thread a little, fill the pumpkin with fleece-wool. Insert the neck into the opening and pull the tacking-thread taut turning the raw edge inwards. Spread out the folds so that the pumpkin becomes nicely rounded and secure the neck. Make embroidered hair (see page 17). Make the stalk by sewing the felt double along its length and sewing it on to the crown of the head. Make a little collar like the real collar of a shirt. Brown eyes suit this pumpkin-child very well.

In the same way you can make all sorts of other fruit-children.

Toadstools

Materials

For a big and a little toadstool.

2 pieces of red felt 2¼" (6 cm) and 3" (8 cm) diameter (the caps)

2 pieces of beige felt of the same size as the red pieces

2 pieces of beige felt 1½" × 3" (4 × 7 cm) and 2¼" × 3" (6 × 7 cm) (the stalks)

A round piece of beige felt ¾" (2 cm) diameter (the feet-pieces)

2 pieces of white felt 3 × 1¼" (7 × 3 cm) (the ring)

Various different and irregular pieces of white felt (the spots)

Little stones to fill the stalk

A piece of lead

Fleece-wool

Figure 43. Toadstool.

Method

Fold the felt for the stalk in half along the width and sew it without a seam with thread of the same colour as the felt. Close up the bottom with the foot-piece. Place a flat piece of lead inside at the bottom of the stalk. Fill the stalk with little stones.

Cut out the circles of the red and beige cap pieces by eye so that they are not perfectly round, and fold the beige cap piece into four and cut out a cross in the middle. Sew the red and the beige layers on to each other and turn the cap through the cut-out cross. Fill the cap lightly with fleece-wool. Sew the cap on to the stalk so that the cut-out cross disappears. Cut the skirt-like ring into points and sew it on to the stalk not quite at the top (Figure 43). Spread the spots over the cap and sew them on.

As the toadstools have to be little toadstool-children, when you are sewing up the stalk you can leave a little opening out of which a tiny face is peeping (Figure 43).

Teasel hedgehog

Materials

A teasel (Latin *Dipsacus fullonum*)

3 pins with black heads

Method

Cut the stalk off the teasel leaving ¼" (5 mm) for the nose. Cut away the long spiky parts round the nose. Make the underside flat by cutting off the spikes with a pair of scissors to stop the hedgehog from rolling over. For the nose stick a black-headed pin into the hollow opening of the cut-off stalk (Figure 44). Stick the other two pins in obliquely above the nose for the eyes. The pins must be inserted right up to their heads into the teasel. If the hedgehog's spikes at the front are standing up too much, clip them off at an angle. The hedgehog should be pointed at the front and round at the back.

Hedgehogs do not like to be on their own!

Figure 44. Teasel hedgehog.

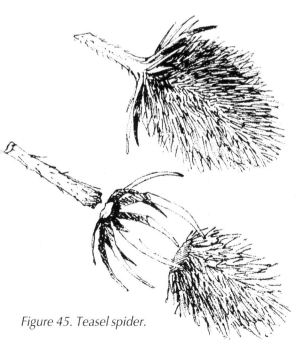

Figure 45. Teasel spider.

Teasel spider

You can easily make a spider from the long underneath spikes of a teasel. First cut off the stalk completely and then cut out the spider from the teasel (Figure 45).

A boy with a kite

The kite is sometimes a symbol of the dragon which makes it appropriate for the season's table at this time of year.

The boy

Materials
Fleece-wool
A piece of thin knitted cotton $4^{1}/_{4}'' \times 4^{1}/_{4}''$ (11 × 11 cm)
A piece of thicker knitted cotton $2^{1}/_{4}'' \times 2^{1}/_{4}''$ (6 × 6 cm)
A scrap of thicker knitted cotton for the hands
6 pipe-cleaners or 2 ft. (60 cm) wire $^{1}/_{32}''$ (0.8 mm) thick
Wool for hair
2.5 mm knitting needles
A bit of matching red wool
Thin brown wool
A suitable crochet hook
A piece of lead flashing
A scrap of felt for the shoes and the scarf

Method
Make a $2^{3}/_{4}''$ (7 cm) head with an eye-line (see page 12) and make hair. The foundation of the body is made from pipe-cleaners or wire.
Cut a piece of wire $12^{1}/_{2}''$ (32 cm) for the body and the legs, and a piece of wire 11″ (28 cm) for the arms.

Bend the wire foundation according to the

diagram (Figure 34). Fix the arms to the body by winding the sticking out pieces of wire round the body. Wrap the skeleton thinly round with sheep's wool leaving ½" (1 cm) of the lower part of the legs free for the feet.

The head can now be set in its place. Cut the knitted cotton of the neck-piece at both sides (Figure 35) and pull it down in front and behind. Tie it firmly under the arms. Fold the thicker knitted cotton for the hands in half. Draw the hands according to the pattern (Figure 35), sew them up, turn them inside out and draw them over the ends of the wire. Tie the hands firmly on to the wrists.

The trousers are crocheted sideways. Make 15 chains, use the first chain for turning. Work 14 double-crochets into this. Take again 1 chain for turning and work 14 double-crochets again. Repeat this till you have made 7 rows. Now make 6 double-crochets and 9 chains. Use the first chain to turn and work 14 double-crochets into the 8 chains and 6 double-crochets. Repeat this till 7 rows are completed and fasten off. Fold the two sides to the middle and sew the inside leg up and then the centre back seam. Tack a thread through the top of the trousers, put the trousers on to the doll, pull in the tacking-thread and so secure the trousers. The trousers come roughly under the arms leaving the feet about ½" (1 cm) uncovered.

The pullover is knitted in one piece with stocking-stitch, that is one row plain, one row purl. These clothes are too small to require ribbing.
Cast on 15 stitches.
Knit 8 rows in stocking-stitch beginning with the a purl row.
Cast on 9 stitches at each end for the sleeves.
Knit 8 rows.
Then cast off the 4 centre stitches.

In the next row cast the centre 4 stitches, but immediately insert the doll into the neck-opening.
Finish the row.
Knit 8 rows.
Cast off 9 stitches at each end.
Knit 8 rows.
Cast off.

Knitting the doll like this is a little awkward but gives a very neat appearance.

Sew up the side seams and the sleeves. Secure the sleeves at the wrists.

Cut out 4 pieces of lead flashing for the feet (Figure 36). Make two holes with a nail in each of two of the pieces. Make the shoes as follows: Cut through the loop of wire at the foot and stick the two ends of the wire through the holes in the lead. This piece of lead then comes directly under the trouser-leg. Bend the wires forward under the lead.

Roll the trouser leg up a bit. Lay the other piece of lead on the piece of felt. Lay them together under the foot, pull the felt well up round the leg, hold it fast there, wind a thread tightly round the ankle and up the leg until the felt is covered, then tie it tight. Roll the trouser leg down over the wound up part of the shoe. (Do not use lead where there are small children, as lead is toxic if licked.)

Finally give the boy a tie from the strip of felt.

The kite

Materials
Cocktail-sticks, lengths 3", 2¼", 1" (8, 5.5, 2.5 cm)
A piece of kite-paper
Thread for the line

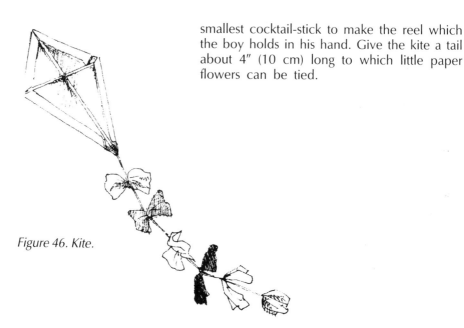

Figure 46. Kite.

smallest cocktail-stick to make the reel which the boy holds in his hand. Give the kite a tail about 4" (10 cm) long to which little paper flowers can be tied.

Method

Lay the two longest cocktail-sticks crosswise on each other. Tie the cross-point firmly. Make little notches at the ends of the sticks to take the stays. Wind the thread round from point to point, each time winding it round the stick into the notch to form the stay strings (Figure 46). Tie the beginning and the end together and cut off the ends. Lay the framework of the kite on the kite-paper. Draw a line round the kite 1/4" (5 mm) outside the stay-string.

Cut out the kite-paper, rounding off the corners. Stick the edges of the kite-paper round the stay-string. Thread a needle with 20" (50 cm) of the thread. Pierce the kite-paper at the cross-point. Draw the thread through the kite-paper, unthread the needle and tie the end of the thread to the cross-point. Now wind the other end of the thread round half of the

The spider in her web

Materials

4 pipe-cleaners 2 3/4" (7 cm)
Some brown unspun sheep's wool
A fresh chestnut
7 bamboo skewers or thin sticks about 10" (25 cm) long
Silver-coloured embroidery-thread

Method

The spider. Wrap one end of the pipe-cleaner with sheep's wool: Use a thin tuft of wool and lay it against the pipe-cleaner, hold it between your forefinger and your middle finger and twist it round the pipe-cleaner. Let go of the tuft, take hold of it again, pull it tight and make another turn round the pipe-cleaner and let go. Keep on working in this way until you have wrapped up one third of the leg. The trick is to keep taking hold of the tuft of wool between your fore and middle finger. As you let go each time the hairs of the wool can become intertwined with the padding of the pipe-cleaner.

Wrap all eight legs up in this way. Lay each pair of legs in a cross and twist them round each other once in the middle. Lay one cross on the other and bind around the middle with wool to make the spider's body. When the spider has been nicely filled you can still mark it with a cross of lighter colour wool.

The web. Take a sharp knife and cut a little slanting notch every 1/2" (1 cm) in the sticks. The notches should slant towards the point of the stick. Stick the points of the sticks all round a chestnut which is lying flat. Tie the silver thread to the notch nearest the chestnut in one of the sticks. Take the thread to the next stick and wind it twice round in the first notch. Continue in this way until you have gone round all the sticks once. Then take the thread to the second notch and go round all the sticks once more. Proceed in this way until all the notches have been filled and the web is complete. Bend the spider's legs and put her in her web.

9. Hallowe'en and Martinmas

Hallowe'en, on October 31, is the night when witches and goblins lose their powers before All Saints' Day. The candles in turnips and pumpkins are like the last memory and afterglow of the summer sun.

A few days later, November 11, is St Martin's Day. Saint Martin was the saint who shared his cloak with a beggar. In some places the children go singing past the doors of the houses with home-made paper lanterns in the evening on St Martin's Day. The people then make the same gesture as St Martin did and give a portion of their harvest.

The paper lantern is like the first glow of a light with a completely different character, the first spark of inner light which ripens towards Christmas.

Lanterns

Turnip lantern (Figure 47)

Materials
A turnip, pumpkin, beetroot or swede
A sharp knife
An apple-corer
A spoon
A little pointed knife
A night-light

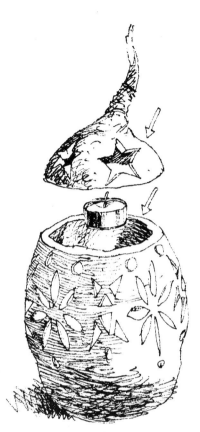

Figure 47. Turnip lantern.

with a spoon. It should be possible to manage with these three tools although the firmness of the turnip can vary considerably.

Once the middle has been removed work carefully towards the outside, pressing your other hand against the outside to gauge the thickness.

As you work hold the lantern up to the light occasionally to see if the wall is thin enough to let the light through. When the wall is nice and thin, you can cut out shapes in the skin, but be careful: cut into the skin of the turnip only, not right through the wall.

The cap of the turnip now becomes the lid, and it also can be hollowed out. An opening in the lid is necessary for ventilation. Place a night light or a candle in a metal container inside the lantern and replace the lid (Figure 47).

This lantern can be preserved a bit longer immersing it in water occasionally.

Method

With a sharp knife cut off a cap from the turnip. If there are no particular marks on the rind you can make a little nick so that you can replace the cap in its right position.

Usually the bottom of the turnip is not level. To make it stand on the seasonal tableau it can be either set in a ring or cut level.

Now we can start hollowing it out. With the apple-corer and the little knife loosen the inside of the turnip so that the pulp can be taken out

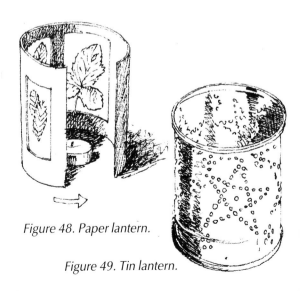

Figure 48. Paper lantern.

Figure 49. Tin lantern.

A simple paper lantern

Materials
A strip of thin cardboard 6″ × 16″ (15 × 40 cm)
Transparent paper (for example grease-proof
    paper)
Dried tree-leaves
A night-light

Method
Cut or prick out one or more windows in the
strip of cardboard. On the back stick a piece of
transparent paper stuck with beautiful dried
leaves. If the openings have attractive forms (as
for instance a star-shape) then transparent
paper is sufficient. Stick the two ends of the
cardboard together to make a cylinder and
place it over the night-light (Figure 48).

A tin lantern

Materials
An empty tin with the top cleanly removed
Nails of various thicknesses, a hammer and a
    pencil
A wooden block
A night-light

Method
Draw some designs on the tin. Punch out the
designs by making holes with the nails. To
preserve the shape of the tin while hammering
in the nails you can put a wooden block inside.
The light of this lantern shines through the holes
(Figure 49).

Gnomes

Nature has often been depicted as having her
special assistants: gnomes. At this time of the
year the gnomes are busy preparing the earth
for the winter, and so they are dressed in
autumn colours. In other seasons a gnome can
wear quite different colours.

Simple felt gnome

Materials
Felt
Well-teased sheep's wool

Method
Fold the felt double and cut out the coat
according to the pattern (Figure 50) without a
seam allowance. Sew up the oblique side of the
pointed cap. Run a gathering thread level with
the neck. Fill the gnome with a smooth tuft of
wool. Draw in the gathering thread and join the
coat together in front. To make the bottom flat
so that the gnome will stand properly, cut level
any protruding wool.

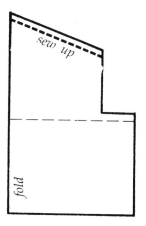

Figure 50. Pattern for a simple gnome.

Tailored felt gnome

Materials

Fleece-wool
A piece of knitted cotton 4″ × 4″ (10 × 10 cm)
A piece of beige thicker knitted cotton 2¼″ ×
    2¼″ (6 × 6 cm)
A scrap of thicker knitted cotton for the hands
2 pipe-cleaners or thin wire
Felt for the clothes and boots
A piece of lead flashing
A length of knitting wool
A tuft of coloured wool for the hair and beard

Method

Make a 2¾″ (7 cm) head with an eye-line and a firm nose (see page 12). Bend in the two ends of a pipe-cleaner to make the arm-piece 4″ (10 cm) long.

Twist the middle of the other pipe-cleaner once all the way round the middle of the arm-piece. Cut into the material of the neck-piece at both sides. Set the head over the cross-point of the pipe-cleaners. Pull the knitted cotton down at the front and back and secure it firmly under the arms.

Double the knitted cotton and draw the hands according to the pattern. Sew them, cut them out with a small seam and turn them. Push both hands on to the ends of the pipe-cleaner and tie them on securely above the wrist. Cut out the clothes according to the pattern (Figure 51) with no seam allowance. Sew the trousers together with little whipping stitches. Put the trousers on the gnome and secure them under the arms. Sew on one shoulder of the smock. Put the smock on the gnome and sew it round the body and arms. Tie a thick strand of knitting wool round his waist as a belt.

For the feet cut out 4 oval pieces of lead (Figure 52). With a nail make a hole in two of the pieces. Stick one pipe-cleaner foot through the hole. Bend the pipe-cleaner under the lead foot, so that the foot comes ¼″ (5 mm) below the leg of the trousers. Make a loop in the end of the pipe-cleaner (cutting off a bit if it is too long). Now place the second piece of lead underneath, and pull a piece of knitted cotton or felt tightly round the foot, stretching the material, and hold it tightly to the leg. Wind a thick strand of wool round the ankle, tie it tight and cut it off in such a way as to make a bootlace. The boot takes shape as you carefully cut off the bits sticking out round the trousers. Make the second boot in the same way.

The eyes and the mouth of the gnome are pulled in and coloured with a light brown crayon. Make hair with a tuft of unspun wool secured here and there. Make the beard by folding a tuft of wool double and securing the fold to the chin.

Sew up the cap. Sew it on to the head securely with little stitches (children will often pick him up by the cap).

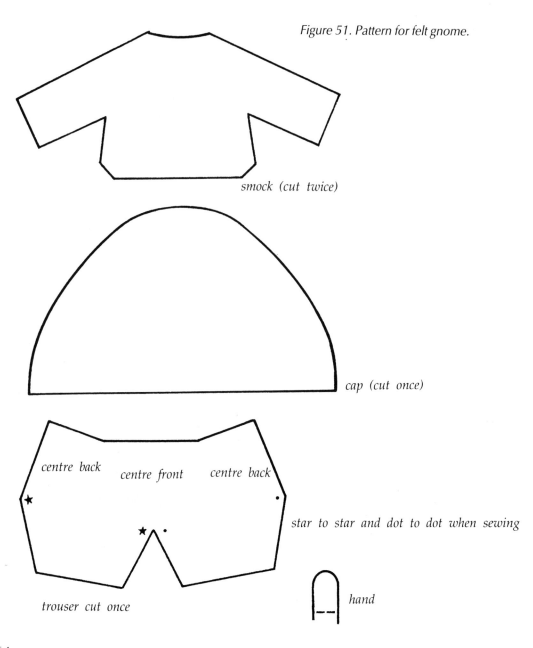

Figure 51. Pattern for felt gnome.

smock (cut twice)

cap (cut once)

centre back   centre front   centre back

star to star and dot to dot when sewing

trouser cut once

hand

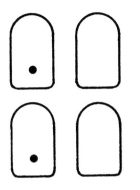

Figure 52. Lead feet.

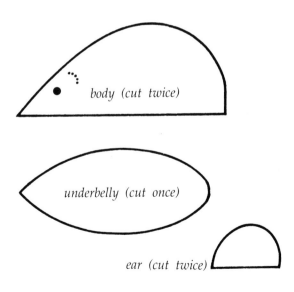

body (cut twice)

underbelly (cut once)

ear (cut twice)

Figure 53. Pattern for a mouse.

A mouse

Materials
A piece of grey felt
A piece of pink felt
Grey embroidery thread
Two little black beads
Fleece-wool or rice

Method
Cut out the body pieces from the grey felt. Cut out the underbelly and the ears from the pink felt according to the pattern (Figure 53). Sew the body-pieces together with little whipping stitches. Sew the underbelly part first to one side of the body with the pointed end to the front, and sew round the back. Fill the mouse with fleece-wool or rice then sew the other side of the belly on to the body. Fold the ear double and fasten it along the fold with a stitch, so that it bulges out a little bit. Sew the ear on to the place indicated on the head. Sew on the two beads for the eyes at the place indicated. This is done best by thrusting the needle through from the back to the eye-socket. Secure at the place for the eye, thread the bead, thrust through the head to the second eye-socket, thread the second bead and secure, then thrust through the body again finally cutting off the two ends of the thread. In this way the ends of the thread are lost in the stuffing of the body and the mouse is finished off neatly.

There remains the tail. Crochet a base-chain 2" (5 cm) long with unsplit embroidery cotton. Pull the thread through the last loop and sew the tail on.

A mouse is rarely alone ...

Figure 54. Advent wreath.

10. Advent

Advent is the time of preparation for Christmas. Advent means literally that which is coming. In order to kindle this mood of expectation the seasonal tableau can be cleared and left completely empty. Only a blue covering indicates that something is coming.

In various ways you can show that the Birth of the Babe is steadily approaching, for example: an Advent calendar with a door to be opened every day until the Child appears on Christmas Eve; Mary and Joseph make a long progress through the room till they arrive at the stable at Christmas; an Advent wreath with four candles for the four Sundays of Advent (one candle is lit on the first Sunday of Advent, two on the second, and so on until all four are lit on the Sunday before Christmas, thus marking the passage of the Advent weeks).

During Advent we can depict the earth's evolution on the seasonal tableau. In the first week we can put on it some beautiful stones. In the second week moss, a fern and a little blossoming plant can be added. In the third week it is the turn of the animals: sheep, an ox and ass. On the fourth Sunday the shepherds appear on the fields, while Mary and Joseph make their way towards the stable.

The angel bringing the Child can descend each day a little nearer to the earth.

The angel

Materials
White teased sheep's wool 14″ (36 cm) long
Gold thread 16″ (40 cm) long

Method
Take a piece of teased sheep's wool 10″ (25 cm) long and about 1″ (3 cm) wide. Tie a knot in the middle and lay the two ends beside each other. The knot forms the head. Tie the neck with the gold thread using the middle of the thread and making the knot behind.

Lay a piece of teased wool 4″ (11 cm) long 1″ (3 cm) wide — for the arms and the wings — between the first two strips under the head. Cross both the left and the right gold threads over the breast. Cross again behind at the waist and again in front at the waist and tie a knot in the middle at the back. From the horizontal piece of wool divide one third for the arms and tie the wrist with gold thread 1¼" (3.5 cm) from the body. Cut off the rest of the wool ¼" (0.5 cm) from the wrist. Fluff the wool lying behind the arms well out for the wings. Fluff the gown well out too.

During Advent you could show the angel carrying the child towards the earth (see page 78). Sew the hands firmly together and lay the child in the angel's arms. After the birth the arms can be spread out. The angel could alternatively have a staff with a star in the hand or a star on the brow.

Saint Nicholas

St Nicholas' day is celebrated on December 6, the beginning of Advent. The great friend of children, St Nicholas visits children at night, and, in their shoes left out in anticipation, puts sweet things for the well-behaved or coal for the naughty. To celebrate this festival is a great preparation for what is coming.

The picture of St Nicholas can be simply presented to a young child, leaving the details to the imagination.

Materials

Teased sheep's wool 2 ft (60 cm)
A piece of red felt, 9" × 6" (23 × 15 cm) (for the cloak)
Another piece of red felt 5" × 2¾" (13 × 7 cm) (for the mitre — St Nicholas was a bishop)
Gold-coloured embroidery thread
A round stick 7" (18 cm) long, ¼" (5 mm) in diameter
A snippet of gold card
Gold paint if required

Method

Tie a knot in the middle of the wool. The knot makes the head. The two strips of wool form the body. Choose one side for the face. On this side pull out a tuft of wool one finger thick for the beard and tie the rest with thread immediately below the knot. Cut the beard to shape.

Cut out the cloak according to the pattern (Figure 55) without a seam allowance and sew up the shoulder seams to the neck edge. Tack along the neck edge, lay the cloak over St Nicholas' shoulders, gather it to a width of 1¼" (3 cm) and sew it on.

Cut out and sew the mitre according to the pattern (centre of Figure 55) and embroider a cross on it with gold thread. Secure the mitre to the head with a few stitches.

Cut out the crook from gold card (Figure 56).

Glue the tab at the base of the crook round the end of the stick and thrust the stick through the slits in the cloak.

St Nicholas' assistant

St Nicholas brings a reward for the good children, but he has a helper who brings retribution to the less well-behaved. In Holland he is called Black Peter.

Materials
A piece of strong card 5½" × 4¾" (14 × 12 cm)
A strip of card 1½" (4 cm) wide
Knitting wool in brown, white and two jolly colours

Method
Wind the brown wool lengthwise round the strong card to the thickness of a finger, then carefully withdraw the card. Tie a thread round the bunch of wool a quarter of the way along its length. This forms the head.

To make the arms, wind one of the coloured wools round the width of the card, until it is half as thick as the body. Withdraw the card carefully. Divide the body into half, back and front. Place the arms between the front and back and tie a thread round the waist. Wind another coloured wool firmly round the wrists to a depth of ½" (1 cm) leaving ½" (1 cm) loops for the hands. Secure the ends under the wound-on wool and cut off. The feet are the same size as the hands. Wind round the bottom of the legs to a depth of 1¼" (3 cm) and finish off as you did for the hands.

Wind the white wool for the collar lengthwise round the 4" (10 cm) card not too close together, then carefully withdraw the card. Lay the loose loops round the doll's neck and tie with a white thread. Fold the collar down. Wind

Figure 55. Pattern for cloak and mitre of St Nicholas.

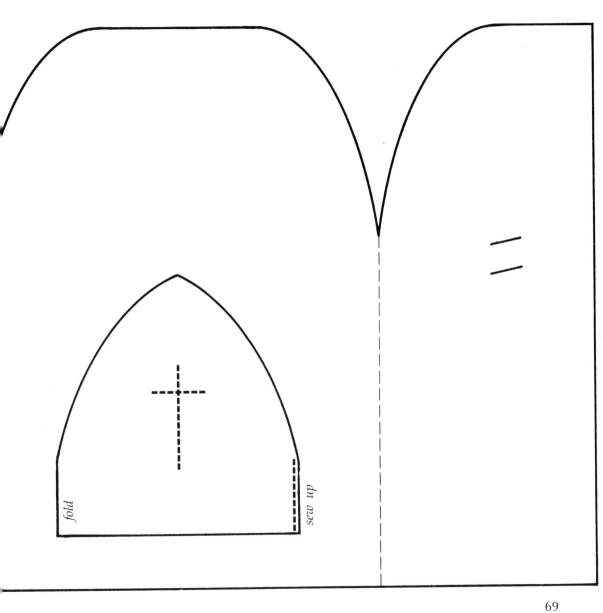

fold

seam up

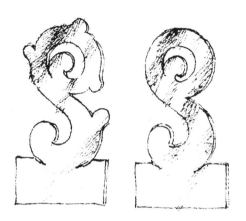

Figure 56. Crook for St Nicholas.

coloured wool round the strip of card one finger thick. Withdraw the card carefully. Make a couple of turns with the end of the wool through the loops and form the wool into a turban-like bonnet. Place the bonnet on the head and sew it on firmly with wool.

The animals

Sheep

Materials
2 pipe-cleaners 2¾" (7 cm) for the legs
A pipe-cleaner 1¼" (3 cm) for the ears
A pipe-cleaner 3¾" (9.5 cm) for head, body
    and tail
Teased wool

Method
Wind fleece wool round the pipe-cleaners. Use a thin tuft of wool and lay it against the pipe-cleaner. Take the tuft firmly between your forefinger and your middle finger and twist it once round the pipe-cleaner. Let go of the tuft, then take it firmly again, pull it and twist it round the pipe-cleaner once again, let go, and continue in this way. This method works well if you take up the tuft of wool each time between your fore and middle finger, and let go each time so that the strands of the wool can become entwined in the padding of the pipe-cleaner and the strands interlock. It is important therefore to work with thin tufts of wool while ensuring the wool does not just become a strand.

Begin the sheep at the head-end. Lay the ear-piece on the longest pipe-cleaner 1¾" (4.5 cm) from the end, and twist it round the wire to make the ears. Now wrap the nose round up to the ears (about ¼", 5 mm thick). Wind round the ears from the top to the middle. Make the middle a bit thicker by winding the wool criss-cross here.

Now bend the head as follows: grip the first ½" (1 cm) between your forefinger and thumb, make a kink and bend the point of the pipe-cleaner in the direction of the point where the ears sit on the head (Figure 58). Now wind over the bent part — the mouth remains free — and shape the head. Attach the leg-part to the body ½" (1 cm) behind the ears with a kink in the middle. Splay the legs out while you are winding on the wool. Start winding at the hoof, the legs becoming thicker as you proceed upwards. The hindlegs are 1½" (3.5 cm) behind the forelegs. Once all four legs and the tail have been wound on, bend the legs down. Bend the upper part of each leg to the width of the body. The lower part of the legs remain straight. Wrap the body well to make it round and soft. Finally bend the tail to hang straight down.

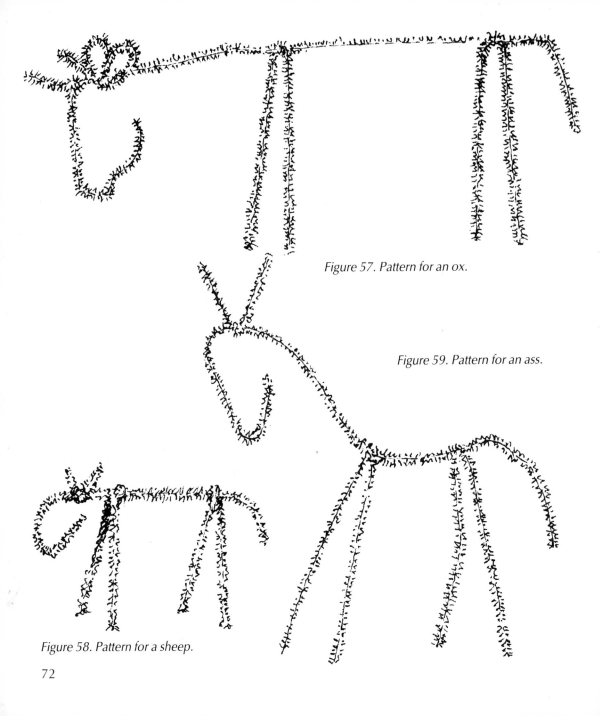

Figure 57. Pattern for an ox.

Figure 59. Pattern for an ass.

Figure 58. Pattern for a sheep.

Ox and ass

Materials
For the ox:
8¼" (21 cm) pipe-cleaner for the head, body
    and tail
2 pipe-cleaners 4¼" (11 cm) long for the legs
A pipe-cleaner 2¼" (6 cm) for the horns
A pipe-cleaner 2¾" (7 cm) for the ears
For the ass:
7" (18 cm) pipe-cleaner for head, body and tail
2 pipe-cleaners 4" (10 cm) for the legs
A pipe-cleaner 2" (5 cm) for the ears
Teased wool the colour of ox and ass

Method
Make the ox and ass in the same way as the
sheep, but of course their posture is different.
The ears are folded in loops. The pipe-cleaners
should be bent according to the diagram
(Figures 57 and 59).

11. Christmas

It is now the darkest time of the year, the days
are short and the nights are long. The earth has
turned in upon itself, it appears bare and empty.
Advent has made us ready, now it is Christmas.
The light has been lit, the days are going to
lengthen, although the difference is as yet
almost unnoticeable.

The expectation has been fulfilled. We add
red, the colour of life, to blue, the colour of
expectation. These are the colours used for
Mary's robe.

Crib figures
Basic method

Mary, Joseph, the shepherds and the kings are
all made according to the basic method.

Materials
Fleece-wool
A piece of thin knitted cotton 4" × 4" (10 × 10
    cm)
A piece of skin-coloured thicker knitted cotton
    2¼" × 2¼" (6 × 6 cm)
A scrap of thicker knitted cotton for the hands
Wool for the hair
A piece of soft card
A piece of cloth for the undergarment a bit
    bigger than the card
A pipe-cleaner
A piece of cloth for the sleeve-piece 4¼" × 2"
    (11 × 5 cm)
Cloth for the cloak
Glue

Method

Make a $2^3/_4''$ (7 cm) head (see page 12). For these crib figures make simple heads with an eye-line only. Draw in the eyes with a coloured pencil, do not make eye-sockets.

The body is made from card. Cut out the card according to the pattern (Figure 61). Cut out the material for the undergarment rather larger than the card. Overlap the projecting edges to the back of the card and glue, so that no glue-marks appear on the front. Insert the head by the neck into the opening of the card having bent the card to a cone with a base of $2^1/_4''$ (6 cm). Staple or sew the two edges firmly together. Allow some glue to run into the cone between the card and the material of the neck and press the material firmly inside the cone.

Bend the pipe-cleaner in at both ends to make the arm-piece $4^1/_4''$ (11 cm) long. Draw the hands according to the pattern on a double thickness of material. Sew them, cut them out and turn. Push the hands on to the ends of the pipe-cleaner and secure at the wrists.

For the sleeves use either the material covering the card or the material of the cloak. Fold the material for the sleeves in half along its length and sew it along the long side to form a tube. Turn the sleeves and push the pipe-cleaner with the hands on it through them. Secure the sleeves at the wrists; you can make a puff-sleeve, a straight sleeve or a wide sleeve. A wide sleeve must be closed so that the construction is not revealed. Staple or sew the sleeve-piece on to the back $1/_2''$ (1 cm) below the neck. Finish the figure with a cloak, a sheepskin or a cap, hat or crown.

The shepherds

Remember shepherds' skin is weather-beaten, their hair is rough, and they often have a beard which are easy to make by folding a tuft of wool over and sewing the folded edge to the chin. They are clad in simple materials, mostly brown-coloured, but in any case use muted colours. Woven fabric and sacking are good materials for this.

The cloaks can be of different kinds: for example a flowing cloak, made of a semi-circular piece 8″ (20 cm) in diameter. Fold the fringes in and secure round the neck, draping the cloak round the body. Hem superfluous material or glue it inside the cone. In this way the cloak can also serve as a cape. To make a proper coat use the same material for the sleeves. The arms stick out through slits cut in the cloak level with the arm-pits. The cloak could even be a blanket loosely slung round, or an animal skin.

Make a cap or hat from knitted material, leather or felt (Figure 60).

The shepherd's crook can be a twig or the stem of a horse-chestnut leaf. Glue or sew the crook on to the shepherd's hand.

A shepherd's bag is a strip of leather or material approx. 2″ × $3/_4''$ (5 × 2 cm) folded in half and stuck together with a shoulder-strap stuck between.

The shepherds can appear in the seasonal tableau on the fourth Sunday of Advent, when their attention is entirely on their sheep. On Christmas morning they come to Mary, Joseph and the Child Jesus. Later they go back to their sheep.

Figure 60. Pattern for cloak, hat and cap of shepherds and kings.

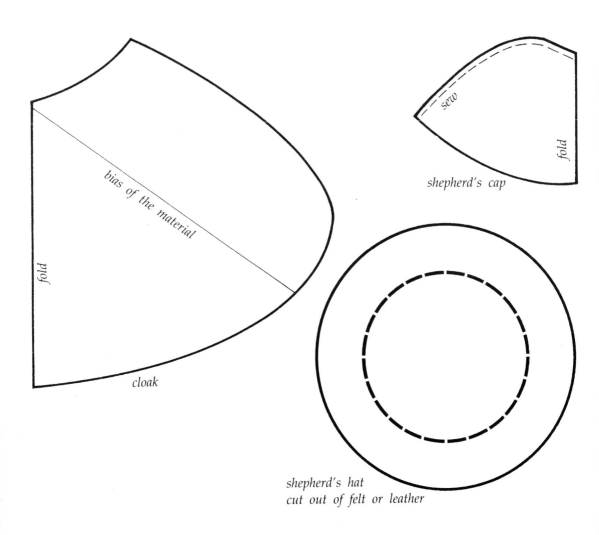

bias of the material

fold

cloak

sew

fold

shepherd's cap

shepherd's hat
cut out of felt or leather

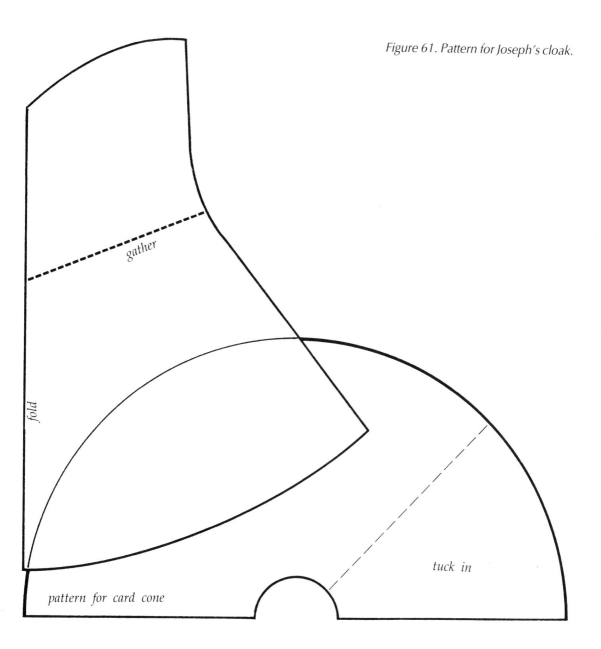

Figure 61. Pattern for Joseph's cloak.

gather

fold

pattern for card cone

tuck in

Joseph

Joseph is distinguished from the shepherds by a smooth brown robe. The robe can be made in the same way as the shepherds' cloaks. Joseph's robe has a hood (Figure 61). Joseph also has a staff in his hand.

Mary

Mary has a fair face and a bright red robe. She does not need any hair as her blue cloak fits exactly round her face. Cut out the cloak according to the pattern (Figure 64) from soft sky-blue material. Tack the U-form according to the pattern but do not draw in the tacking thread yet. Lay the cloak with a little fold tight against the forehead at point A (Figure 62) and sew it on behind the neck. Bring the two folds at the side of the head down in front of the ears to meet under the chin. Pull the cloth up a bit at the centre-back by pulling in the tacking thread right to the neck and secure according to the sketch at point B. Drape the material round Mary, taking care that there is enough room for her to hold her child in her arms. The red robe remains visible in front. Secure the cloak at the wrists, again making a little fold. Hem the loosely hanging material with little stitches or fold the bottom edge in under the cone and glue it there.

The Child

Tie a knot in a piece of teased sheep's wool ¼" (0.5 cm) wide. Fold the wool double, the knot makes the head. Trim the body to a length of 1" (2.5 cm). Arrange a piece of material 4" × 4" (10 × 10 cm) (preferably pastel-coloured silk) around the head as described for Mary. Wrap the body up by folding the cloth in a cocoon shape measuring 1¼" (3 cm). Sew the body with little stitches (Figure 63).

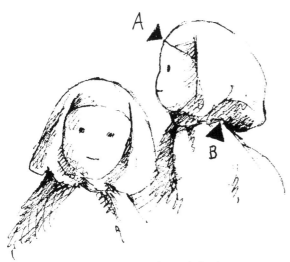

Figure 62. Mary's draped cloak.

Figure 63. The Child.

The three kings

On January 6 the magi, kings from distant lands, come to Mary, Joseph and the Child. They have found their way to the stable following the star. King Melchior, traditionally the first, has a red mantle and a grey beard. His gift is red gold. King Balthazar, the eldest, has a blue mantle. His gift is frankincense. King Caspar is the black king. He has a green mantle. His gift is myrrh.

Each of the three kings has a white robe. Cut the mantles according to the pattern (Figure 60) using a rich material, for example velvet, felt or silk. Velvet is very thick and difficult to hem, so it is better to turn the edges under and stick them with some textile adhesive. Felt does not need to be hemmed. The mantles can be trimmed with gold thread.

The gifts can be: a little copper bell, a round bulgy button, a tiny coloured ball from the Christmas Tree, a little box made of gold paper, a toy cup painted gold, gold painted acorns, alder-cones or eucalyptus fruit.

Once the three wise kings have departed, Mary, Joseph and the Child Jesus set off on their way to Egypt, and so slowly disappear from the seasonal tableau.

The star which showed the way to the kings shines till February 2, Candlemas.

Figure 64. Pattern of Mary's cloak.

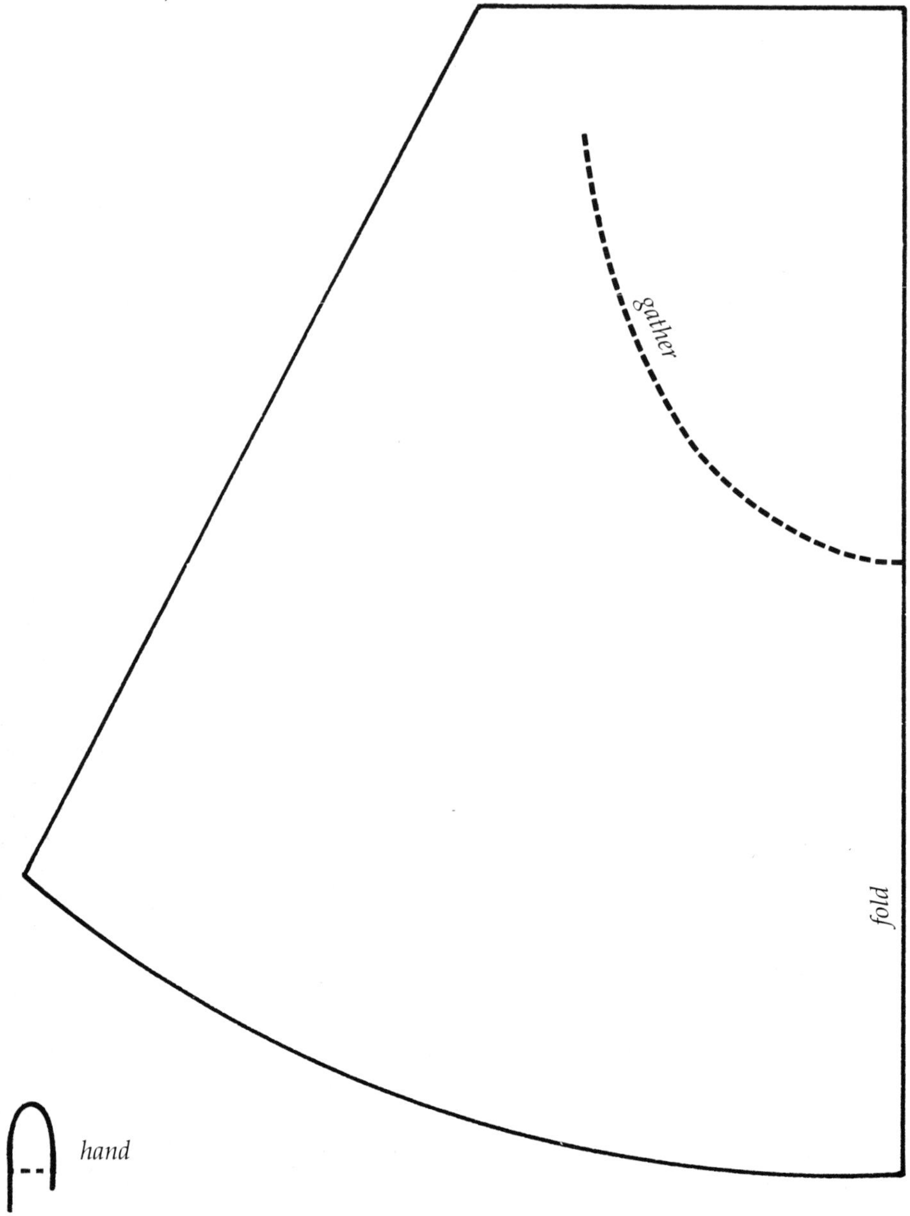

gather

fold

hand

12. Winter

When the snow comes and the earth is covered with a white mantle it is clear that King Winter's rule has begun. Frost makes the air clear and snowflakes come floating down like little crystalline stars. Children enjoy every moment out of doors, because before you know Mrs Thaw comes along with her broom to spoil the fun!

King Winter

Materials

A piece of thin knitted cotton 6″ × 6″ (15 × 15 cm)

A piece of pale pink thicker knitted cotton 4″ × 3¼″ (10 cm × 8.5 cm)

A scrap of pale pink thicker knitted cotton for the hands

Fleece-wool

A stand 6″ (15 cm) high (see page 11)

Wire 16″ (40 cm) long, ¹/₃₂″ (0.8 mm) thick

A piece of white or grey material 12½″ × 8¾″ (32 × 22 cm) for the robe

A piece of white woolly material 16″ × 12″ (40 × 30 cm) for a cloak with a train, or a piece of felt 10¼″ × 6″ (26 × 15 cm) for a cloak with icicles

A round piece of material for the undergarment 10½″ (26.5 cm) diameter.

Carded unspun white wool for the hair

A piece of silver card 6″ × 2″ (15 × 5 cm)

A piece of silver paper 2¾″ × 2″ (7 × 5 cm)

Method

Make a 4¾″ (12 cm) doll's head (see page 12). Place the head on the stand and tie the scraps of material from the head with a thread tightly round the stand. Push the thread through the hole so that the head is secure. Check the total height which should be 7″ (18 cm). Make the arms by bending the ends of the wire back to the middle. The arm-piece should be 7″ (18 cm) long. Sew the middle of the wire firmly to the back about ½″ (1 cm) below the head. Wrap the arms round with fleece-wool to fill them out.

Draw the hands according to the pattern (Figure 65) on a double thickness of material. Sew them and turn them, fix the hands on to the arm-pieces and secure them to the wrists.

Run a gathering thread along the undergarment ½″ (1 cm) from the edge. Place the stand on the centre of the material and gather the tacking thread. Secure the undergarment at the waist.

Cut out the robe according to the pattern (Figure 65) with a small hem allowance. Sew up the sides of the sleeves. Run a gathering thread round just below the neck, put the robe on King Winter, pull up the gathering thread round the neck turning the raw edge inside and secure the robe. Turn under a small hem for the sleeves and sew them round the wrists. Hem the robe.

Choose a cloak with a train or one with icicles. For the cloak with a train cut a piece of cloth 12″ (30 cm) wide, round off the corners and hem. Cut out the cloak with icicles according to the pattern (Figure 66). Gather the top of both cloaks and secure them round the neck.

Now make the eyebrows, moustache and beard of ice. These are made of little tufts of

unspun wool. Do not cut the tufts, but tease them out. This makes the hair more attractive. Fold the tufts over, hold them securely and sew them on.

To make the hair tease out a tuft of white wool about 8″ (20 cm) long. Place the middle of this on top of the head and sew a parting with embroidery stitches on top only, so that the hair can easily be parted.

Cut out the crown according to the pattern (Figure 65) or according to your own design. Glue it together to fit the King and place it on his head.

Draw light blue eyes for the king.

His sceptre is a piece of silver paper rolled round a little stick. The stick can be removed afterwards. Sew the sceptre to his right hand. In his left hand King Winter holds the orb, a snowball made of a tightly-rolled sewn ball of wool.

Now King Winter can mount his throne.

Mrs Thaw

Whenever Mrs Thaw gets the chance she will sweep the snow to one side. At first King Winter cannot be swept away, he simply snows everything under again. In the end King Winter however has to go back to the High North.

In spring Mrs Thaw sweeps all the snow and ice away. Wearing a clean apron, she wakes the springtime fairy once again.

Materials
Fleece-wool
A piece of soft thin knitted cotton 6″ × 6″ (15 × 15 cm)
A piece of salmon-coloured thicker knitted cotton 4″ × 3¼″ (10 × 8.5 cm)
A scrap of thicker knitted cotton for the hands
A wooden stand 5½″ (14 cm) high (see page 11)
Wire 16″ (40 cm) long, ¹/₃₂″ (0.8 mm) thick
Grey-brown knitting wool for the hair
Use grey colours for the clothing:
Blouse 8¾″ × 6¼″ (22 × 16 cm)
Skirt 15″ × 5½″ (38 × 14 cm)
Apron 4¼″ × 4¼″ (11 × 11 cm) with a string 8¾″ × 1¼″ (22 × 3 cm)
Another apron in fresh colours
A piece of cloth for the cloak 10″ × 5″ (25 × 13 cm)
A piece of cloth for the hood 6¼″ × 2¾″ (16 × 7 cm)
A press-stud
A scrap of the same cloth as the cloak
A bit of beeswax (modelling wax) for the shoes
Twigs for the broom
A piece of fine fuse wire

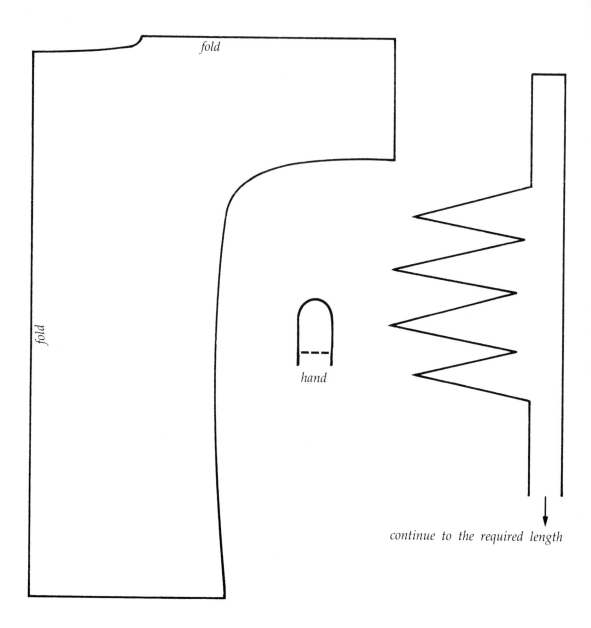

fold

fold

hand

continue to the required length

Figure 65. Pattern of King Winter's robe.

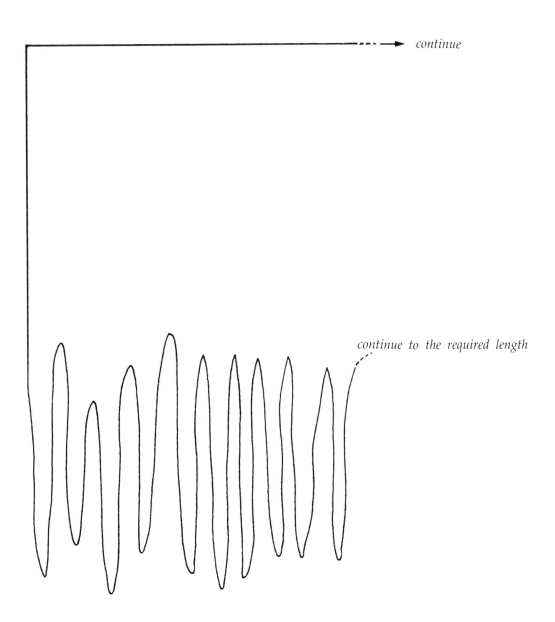

continue

continue to the required length

Figure 66. Pattern of King Winter's icicle cloak.

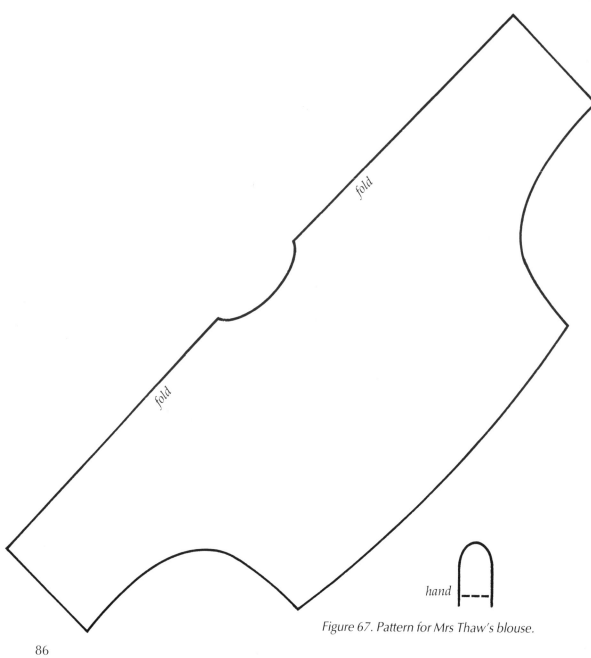

fold

fold

hand

Figure 67. Pattern for Mrs Thaw's blouse.

Method

Make a 4¾" (12 cm) head. Mrs Thaw can have lines round her mouth and a nose. Place the head on the stand and tie the scraps of material from the head to the stand with thread, running the thread through the hole in the stand so that the head is secure. Check the overall height which should be 7" (18 cm).

Make the arm pieces by bending back the ends of the wire to the middle so that the piece is 7" (18 cm) long. Sew the middle of the wire firmly on to the back about ½" (1 cm) below the head.

Wrap the arms round with fleece-wool to fill them out.

Draw the hands according to the pattern (Figure 67) on a double thickness of material, sew them, Cut them out and turn them.

Push the hands over the ends of the arm-pieces and secure them at the wrists.

Cut out the blouse according to the pattern (Figure 67) with a small seam allowance. Sew the blouse, cut open the centre-back. Gather the neck opening with a little hem right round, leaving the thread hanging. Put the blouse on Mrs Thaw, draw up the thread round the neck and fasten on. Sew up the centre-back. Fasten the gathered sleeves round the wrists. Cut out the skirt and hem the bottom edge. Sew up the back and tack the top with a double thread, turning in the raw edge. Put the skirt on over the blouse, pulling up the tacking thread and secure. Hem the apron along both sides and the bottom. Gather the top. Lay the mid-point of the string to the mid-point of the apron and sew it on along the top edge of the apron. Fold the top over the string and hem it. Make the second apron in the same way.

Make the hair as follows: From the knitting wool cut strands 9½" (24 cm) long, sufficient to cover the top of the head. Lay the wool over the top of the head, thread a needle with a length of wool work a parting with embroidery stitches. Let a few hairs hang untidily over her face. Make a bun at the back of her head by bringing the strands round to the back and twisting them. Secure the bun with a few stitches. Hem the sides and bottom of the cloak. Gather the top edge. Hem a long edge of the hood to make the front. Fold the cloth widthways and sew up the back. Lay the gathered edge of the cloak to the neck edge of the hood and sew it on. Make a tab from a scrap of material and sew it on to the cloak under the chin, sew a press-stud on to it. The cloak must be removed when spring comes.

Make a pair of sturdy shoes from modelling wax and stick them on to the front of the base of the stand.

The broom is made of a 6" (15 cm) stick with various twigs measuring 3" (7 cm). Fasten the twigs to the broom with wire and sew it into Mrs Thaw's hands.

Mrs Thaw sweeps the earth clean. Then Mother Earth wakes her root-children deep under the ground among the roots of the trees ...

Bibliography

Berger, Thomas, *The Christmas Craft Book,*
　　Floris 1990.
Beskow, Elsa, *Around the Year,* Floris 1988.
—, *Children of the Forest,* Floris 1987.
—, *The Flower Festival,* Floris 1991.
—, *Ollie's Ski Trip,* Floris 1989.
—, *Pelle's New Suit,* Floris 1989.
—, *Woody, Hazel and Little Pip,* Floris 1990.
Bittleston, Adam, *Meditative Prayers for Today,*
　　Floris 1988.
Capel, Evelyn, *The Christian Year,* Floris 1982.
Carey, D. and J. Large, *Festivals, Family and
　　Food,* Hawthorn Press.
Cooper, S., C. Fynes-Clinton and M. Rowling,
　　The Children's Year, Hawthorn Press.
Jaffke, Freya, *Toymaking with Children,* Floris
　　1988.
Jones, Michael, *Prayers and Graces,* Floris
　　1987.
Olfers, Sibylle von, *The Story of the Root
　　Children,* Floris 1990.
Reinckens, Sunnhild, *Making Dolls,* Floris 1989.
Steiner, Rudolf, *The Cycle of the Year,*
　　Anthroposophic Press.
—, *The Festivals and their Meaning,* Rudolf
　　Steiner Press.
Verschuren, I. *The Christmas Story Book,* Floris
　　1988.